To:

From:

Date:

NIV Adventure BIBLE

Book of Devotions

POLAR EXPLORATION EDITION

NIV
Adventure BIBLE

Book of
Devotions

365 DAYS of DEVOTIONS

ZONDER**kidz**™

POLAR EXPLORATION EDITION

ZONDERKIDZ

NIV Adventure Bible Book of Devotions: Polar Exploration Edition
Copyright © 2018 by Zondervan
Illustrations © 2018 by Zondervan

This title is also available as a Zondervan ebook.

Requests for information should be addressed to:
Zonderkidz, *3900 Sparks Dr. SE, Grand Rapids, Michigan 49546*

ISBN 978-0-31076500-4 (hardcover)

ISBN 978-0-310-765073 (epub)

Published in association with the Books & Such Literary Management, 52 Mission Circle, Suite 122, PMB 170, Santa Rosa, California 95409-5370, www.booksandsuch.com.

Zonderkidz is a trademark of Zondervan.

Content by: Rebekah Hamrick Martin
Interior design: Denise Froehlich

Printed in China

18 19 20 21 22 /DSC/ 10 9 8 7 6 5 4 3 2 1

Introduction

AdVenTuring wiTh Jesus

Imagine traveling to a place you've always dreamt of visiting—you could get there by hiking with your feet, soaring through the air on an airplane, or bumping through the desert on a bus. You can't believe you finally get to check out the place you've always wanted to visit! You're not sure what will happen along your journey, but you know it's going to be an adventure.

Imagine this book as an adventure you get to take with God. Each page you turn will take you someplace you might not have expected to go. You know your destination: getting closer to Jesus. But you never know what kinds of twists and turns will take you to that destination. It only takes a few minutes each day to get there. Enjoy this journey, and maybe even share it with a friend. You'll be glad you took this adventure with Jesus.

This Is Your Adventure!

Have I not commanded you? Be strong and courageous. Do not be afraid; do not be discouraged, for The Lord your God will be with you wherever you go.

—Joshua 1:9

What scares you the most in life? What's that one thing you'd never tell your friends about because, hey, it's just not cool to screech like a hyena on a roller coaster? What dreams keep you awake at night, but you just can't bring yourself to go after them? Maybe you want to try out for the lead role. Maybe you want to talk to a new person at school. Maybe you want to run for class president.

God says to be courageous about that. He says go after your dreams. He says not to be afraid. But what does that look like? Can you tell your heart to stop beating so fast and your adrenaline to stop pumping through your veins? No, being courageous is taking one small step toward your dream. It's about taking one step after that and another step after that. With God on your side, you can be strong and courageous for this adventure he has planned for you—no matter how it turns out!

Write down a dream you have that you've been too scared to pursue. Then write down the steps you would take to make that dream come true.

Take that first step. God is with you.

DAY 2

Take the Leap

Whoever is kind to the poor lends to the Lord, and he will reward them for what they have done.

PROVERBS 19:17

Did you have a good day yesterday? Or was it a bad one? Did you make the basket at the basketball game or did you fail the test? Were your friends in a good mood, or did they tease you in class about your crush? Good things happen some days, and bad things happen some days. The same thing is true for everyone—but it seems like some people have more bad days than good ones.

Look around you today. Who's having a bad day or even a lot of bad days? There are people all around us who are struggling. It might be someone at school, or it might be someone you've never met. Is there a way you can make someone else's day, or even life, better? Is there a volunteer group at school or church you can join? It could be a huge adventure for you—feeding the homeless at the shelter (if it's okay with your parents), walking someone's dog, or even helping someone cross the street. You could change someone's day—even their life—with the actions you choose to take.

Sometimes it's good to start small—what's one thing you could do to make a difference today? Ask the adult in your life for permission, and then sign up to do something for someone else. You might even find that it makes you happier inside!

It's All about the Thumbs

But love your enemies, do good to them, and lend to them without expecting to get anything back. Then your reward will be great, and you will be children of the most high, because he is kind to the ungrateful and wicked.

LUKE 6:35

Do you have a cell phone? Do you have a computer or use the laptop at the library? No matter where you go, it's hard to escape social media. It seems like all your classmates are posting, updating, and commenting on every moment. It's easy for both good news and embarrassing photos to make it around the school in a matter of moments.

The question is: how will you choose to use social media? When someone posts an embarrassing photo of you, will you dig up dirt and do it right back? After all, they deserve it, right? Well . . . maybe not. It's not fair what they did to you, but as the saying goes, two wrongs do not make a right. Instead of returning the favor to spark a full-on Internet war, think of something good you can do for the person who embarrassed you. And if you keep running into trouble with a person or group of people online, talk to an adult or look for new friends to spend time with.

Look at your hands today. God gave you eight fingers and two thumbs. What will you choose to do with those thumbs today? Ask God to give you the strength to choose love—because love goes a long way in changing the world.

You Fit Here

BUT now, This is what The Lord says—he who created you, Jacob,
he who formed you, Israel: "Do not fear, for I have redeemed you;
I have summoned you by name; you are mine."

ISAIAH 43:1

Do you ever feel like no one in the whole world is paying attention to you? Maybe your family is super-busy, or your friends are making plans that simply don't involve you (ouch). Maybe it feels like there's nowhere you belong.

Do you know something? You are valuable to God. If you could see him, you would know that Jesus is with you right now. He says he's the one who will never leave you—he's the one you can really count on. He wants to hear your thoughts, prayers, worries, and hopes. If he had a smartphone, he'd be calling you up, wanting to chat, wanting you to know—I like you. I made you. And I call you my own.

So next time you're wondering if you're invisible, know that God loves you. He won't abandon you. He won't leave you alone.

When you feel left out, try this prayer: Jesus, I'm feeling like no one notices me. But you promise that you do. Help me to trust your plan for me, and help me to know I'm never alone. Help me to trust you and know that you are here. In Jesus' name, amen.

That "O" Word

Children obey your parents in the Lord, for this right. "Honor your father and your mother."

EPHESIANS 6:1–2A

What's the last fight you had with the adult in your life? Was it over what you wanted to wear, who you wanted to hang out with, or even whether you wanted to roll out of bed to get to school? (Speaking of rolling, did you roll your eyes at them?) One of the toughest verses in the Bible to swallow (worse than split pea soup) is the one that says we should honor the adults in our lives, especially the ones we live with. Those adults aren't perfect, and sometimes it makes absolutely no sense what they're asking us to do.

But most of us live with safe adults—adults who want the best for us and are trying their hardest to make life go well for us. Most parents and guardians are helping you prepare for the future. When they ask you to do your homework, clean out the litter box, or stay away from the mean crowd, they're helping you gear up for the adventure of adulthood. They want you to be prepared.

What's one way you can show respect to the adult you live with today? Write down the way you can honor your guardians today.

The Hole in Your Sock

The eyes of The Lord are on The righteous, and his ears are attentive to their cry.

PSALM 34:15

Prayer takes faith. Faith means it takes believing that God is listening even when he seems far away. There was a man in the Bible who told Jesus, "I believe—help my unbelief." If you're having trouble believing that God hears you today, it's okay to tell him that. It's okay to say, "God, I'm worried about this science test—it's freaking me out. And really, I'm having trouble believing that you care about such a little thing."

God does care about the little things and the big things. He cares about your paper cut, and he cares about your parents' divorce. He cares about that fight with your best friend, and he cares about the hole in your sock. He wants to hear about everything—he's just waiting for you to tell him.

Think of something that's bothering you today. It might be big, or it might be small. Can you tell God about that one thing? Every time you ask him to help you with something in your life, it builds your faith and helps you take the next step on the adventure he has for you.

Valuable to God

... The Lord does not look at the things people look at. People look at the outward appearance, but the Lord looks at the heart.

I Samuel 16:7b

Some people are going to tell you that you aren't valuable enough. That you don't look good enough. That your brain's not smart enough. Let me tell you a secret: some people act this way because they feel very unsure of themselves.

Nothing you do or do not do on this adventure with God will add or subtract from your value with him. You cannot disappoint your heavenly father, because disappointment comes from surprise, and God is never surprised. The one who made you—God—says you are wonderful. He made the outside and the inside of who you are. And he says that because of Jesus, you are just right—you are more than enough!

Can you thank God today for making you more than enough because of Jesus? Thank him for the power that lives inside you and gives you strength to believe that he made you valuable, just the way you are.

Beware of the Frenemies

Walk with the wise and become wise, for a companion of fools suffers harm.

PROVERBS 13:20

Do you have a friend who does everything with you— sits at the lunch table, plays on the same sports team, even goes to the same church? But maybe, even though you are super close to this friend, he is always putting you down. When you walk away from talking with your friend you don't feel better about yourself. You feel much, much worse.

Maybe you keep hanging out with this person because you've always been friends, or maybe you keep hanging out because you're worried about what will happen if you no longer have that friendship. Maybe being around your friend feels like wearing an old pair of jeans, comfortable and familiar—until it's not. Does this person talk about you behind your back? Do they say mean things about you to your face?

Today is a new day, and God says you don't deserve to be treated like that. You're his child, and you shouldn't be afraid to stand up for yourself.

Talk with an adult you trust about how your friend is treating you. If you need to, confront your friend. Tell him that if his behavior doesn't change, you can't hang out anymore. Stay true to your word—this person might not be happy, but you're doing the right thing by treating yourself the way God treats you.

Embarrassed on Television

For we do not have a high priest who is unable to empathize with our weaknesses, but we have one who has been tempted in every way, just as we are—yet he did not sin.

HEBREWS 4:15

It's on all the time when you're flipping channels (if you can pry the remote from your brother's hands): reruns of shows where people do embarrassing things. People on TV are slipping, falling, even skiing into boulders. Sometimes their pants fall down, or they get caught air-guitaring in the mirror with only a towel wrapped around their waists.

Why would anyone agree to let their most embarrassing moments air on television? Mostly because the person who has the funniest (or sometimes most embarrassing) movies wins money—and lots of it.

You're not going to win any money when you fall over your shoelaces at school, or when you drop your lunch tray all over yourself. Embarrassing things happen every day, and other people love to remind you about them. But you know what? Jesus is no stranger to being laughed at, or embarrassed. He lived here on earth and experienced all the emotions and situations we do. He is with you, and he understands. He wants to help you feel better and move on.

Think about something embarrassing that's happened in your life. Picture Jesus with you, telling you he understands how it feels. He has a box in his hands—can you put all those feelings there? He'd love to take them for you.

Winning the Argument

Be kind and compassionate to one another, forgiving each other, just as in Christ God forgave you.
EPHESIANS 4:32

When you're in the middle of an argument—one where you know you're right—the last thing you want to do is give up and apologize. But you know what? Giving up and apologizing aren't the same thing. In fact, God wants us to forgive people freely—even the people we're arguing with.

It might make you feel a little angry to learn that God says to forgive your enemies. Doesn't he understand how much it hurts? Doesn't he care that someone could be so cruel? The answer is, yes! He cares so very much. In fact, he wants you to forgive not so that your enemy can feel better—but so that you can feel better. When you forgive the person who hurt you, it allows you to focus on other things instead of filling your head with thoughts about what happened.

Forgiveness doesn't mean you have to allow that person to treat you badly again (it's important to stand up for yourself!), but it does mean that you can keep giving God the pain of what that person did every time your mind tries to bring it up again. You can tell God all about it. He can help.

Is there someone in your life you need to forgive? If this person is hurting your body or mind, you need to tell a safe adult. But if the forgiveness is for something else, try this prayer: Dear God, I give you my frustration. I know you understand how it feels. I choose to forgive because you forgave me and want to help me. In Jesus' name, amen.

Who Took Out the Trash?

One of Them, when he saw he was healed, came back, praising God
in a Loud voice. He Threw himself at Jesus' feet and Thanked him.

LUKE 17:15–16A

Have you ever done something nice for someone and they didn't even notice? Maybe you made your sister's bed or took out the trash and no one said a word. Some jobs are what people call "thankless" because people just expect them to happen. After all, when was the last time you said thanks to the person who picks up the trash from your curb? What if he or she just left it rotting there for weeks? Or when was the last time you said thanks to your dentist? (More like "no thanks!") Who needs their teeth checked, anyway . . . until that tooth falls out.

Did you know that Jesus healed ten people from a terrible disease in one day, and only one of those people came back to thank him? They may have been so excited to be healed that they forgot to say, "Wow, thanks!" Sometimes when good things happen in our lives, it's easy to forget to thank God for making those good things happen. But he is our father and he deserves our thanks!

What's one good thing that's happened to you this week? Did you remember to thank God for it? If not, close your eyes and do so now.

Show Me the Money

No one can serve two masters. Either you will hate the
one and love the other, or you will be devoted to the one
and despise the other. You cannot serve both God and money.
MATTHEW 6:24

What's the most money you've ever had at one time? Did you spend it? Did you save it? Did you give it away? Money can be an important thing, and it's easy to sit and daydream about what you'd buy if you had a lot of it. People spend a lot of time chasing cash, and there's nothing wrong with having financial security. But God says there is something wrong with loving money more than loving him.

How do you know if you love money more than you love God? You might spend more time thinking about cash than you do thinking about him, or you might hold your savings so close that you're not willing to share with others who need help. When you see a fundraiser at school to help the homeless, what's your first thought? When your youth leader is raising money to go on a mission trip, are you willing to pitch in?

Money is a special gift from God, especially when it's used in a way that honors him.

Write down some ways that you can earn money, and then some ways that you can share some of what you earn. You could be a huge blessing in someone's life just by giving some of what God's given you.

Finding Your Glue

And Let us consider how we may spur one another on toward love and good deeds, not giving up meeting together, as some are in the habit of doing, but encouraging one another—and all the more as you see the Day approaching.

HEBREWS 10:24–25

Do you have a best friend? Someone you want to spend all your time with? Do you share the same interests, like hiking, exploring, or playing volleyball? Maybe you have gaming marathons or campouts under the stars. Whatever they are, those interests are like glue that holds your friendship together.

God says that he's the glue that should hold some of your friendships together too. Having friends who love him and want to know him more helps us stay strong in our faith. That's why the Bible says we should hang out with people who love God, and a great place to do that is church or youth group.

If you don't have a church or youth group yet, ask the adult in your life if you can find one. Make sure that you feel safe and welcomed by the people who are there. If the first place you visit isn't right for you, keep looking and you'll find just the right place (you might even have an after-school Christian group at your school that you don't even know about)! No church group is perfect, but you can find the place where you fit best.

If you don't have a church or youth group to attend, find out if you can visit some this weekend. If you do attend a church or youth group, don't forget to keep going and making more friends. The church is an important part of your life that helps you keep learning more about God.

You Bought It at the Thrift Store

These are The Things you are To do: Speak TruTh To each oTher, and render True and Sound judgmenT in your courTs; do noT ploT evil againsT each oTher, and do noT swear falseLy . . .

ZECHARIAH 8:16-17A

Everyone "stretches the truth" at one point or another— maybe it's when you're telling a story to your friends and you make it sound just a little better than what actually happened. Maybe you tell your parents you came home at 9:00 like they asked, but it was actually 9:15. Maybe you say you bought your shirt at the mall when it actually came with the new tags on it from the thrift store.

It's tempting to let "little" lies sneak into our conversations, but God holds us to a higher standard of truth. Because he loves us, he wants us to be like him. None of us other than Jesus is perfect, but with a little bit of practice and the help of the Holy Spirit, we can become truth-tellers. How? Next time you find yourself telling a "little" lie, pause and think. Then open your mouth and tell the truth instead. Soon you'll find that other people trust you more—and you might even stand up a little taller.

What are some areas of your life where you tend to bend the truth? What can you do to change that the next time you're tempted to slip in that little white lie? Keep a journal of all the times God's helped you tell the truth.

Why Doesn't He Fix It?

TrusT in The Lord wiTh all your heart and lean not on your own understanding; in all your ways submit to him, and he will make your paths straight.

PROVERBS 3:5-6

Sometimes it seems like there's bad news all around you—on social media, television, and even in your own life. Good things happen, but terrible things happen sometimes too. It's a sad part of this broken world we live in. It's hard to watch and even harder to live through.

God says he is with you in your bad news. Whether it came on suddenly or slowly, your pain is not a surprise to him. The one who made you knew exactly when and how this would happen, and his heart breaks that it did. You might have a few questions, like, if he's so powerful, why doesn't he just fix it? Why did he allow it in the first place?

The Bible says there are a lot of things we can't see—a lot of things we don't yet understand. But it also says that one day you will understand. Until that day comes, remember God promises that when you talk to him about what you don't understand, he'll be there to guide and help you.

Do you need to talk with someone today? Sometimes when life gets painful, it helps to talk with an adult who can pray for you and listen. Can you find that person? If you don't know anyone like that, keep praying and looking. God is watching out for you.

No More Baby Face

BuT grow in The grace and knowLedge of our Lord and Savior
Jesus ChrisT. To him be gLory boTh now and forever! Amen.
2 Peter 3:18

Have you ever watched a baby learn to walk? Maybe it was your brother or sister or your cousin. It's hard work for a baby to build those muscles and figure out how to put one foot in front of the other. You may have even watched that baby fall on her face again and again! But after a few weeks, then a few months, it's like the kid had always been walking—you couldn't even tell he or she had to practice so much. That baby is growing up.

You're growing up too. There are lots of things you can do now that you weren't always able to—you can play rough sports, read huge books, and go new places on your own. Did you know God wants you to grow up in knowing him too? He doesn't want you to stay like a tiny baby, always needing an adult to tell you what you need to know about him and the Bible. He wants you to read his Word and know him for yourself, every day if you can. When you practice studying the Bible and praying, you're like a baby taking steps—steps that will one day lead you to exciting places you can't even imagine.

The more you grow in God, the more you can share what you learn with others. Even though you're growing, you'll still want help sometimes. Write down three questions about God you can ask an adult you know. The more you know, the more you grow!

Don't Wash Out

No TempTaTion has overTaken you excepT whaT is common To mankind. And God is faiThful; he will noT LeT you be TempTed beyond whaT you can bear. BuT when you are TempTed, he will also provide a way ouT so ThaT you can endure iT.

1 CORINTHIANS 10:13

When lightning crashes and wind blows and rain pours, dangerous things can happen. One of those dangerous things is flooding—rivers, lakes, and streams can spill over their banks into places they shouldn't be. People, cars, and even houses can be washed away.

God gives us boundaries too. He asks us to stay inside of those boundaries—like listening to our parents, not cheating in school, and making good decisions. He also gives us those boundaries so we can stay safe. Sometimes our friends might want us to do something we know is risky, like sneaking into an R-rated movie or going to a party where there are no adults. Whatever the temptation, it can feel hard to say no when everyone else is doing it. Next time you feel like doing something dangerous just because your friends are trying it, remember that God wants to protect you from that storm. Ask him for the power to say no, and talk to an adult you can trust.

Make a plan for what you'll do if your friends ask you to do something you know is a bad idea. You don't want to be a snitch, but you do want to keep your friends safe. It might mean texting or calling a safe adult and asking them to help you get out of that situation!

Where's Your Spotlight?

Anger is cruel and fury overwhelming, but who can stand before jealousy?

PROVERBS 27:4

What are you good at? Is it playing an instrument? Sports? Art? Are you good at helping others? Or maybe you're a good listener?

Has anyone ever been jealous of those things you can do? Maybe they said something unkind or whispered about you behind your back. They might not have realized it, but they were probably envious of what you've accomplished or what you have.

Jealousy can go both ways, though. Someone can be jealous of you, and you can be jealous of someone else. Envy is a normal emotion—it's just part of being human. But it's important that we don't stay jealous or hurt others because of how we're feeling. Do you know the best way to cure that jealous feeling? Thanking God for the abilities and possessions he's given you. The more you focus your spotlight on what gifts *you* have (especially the best gift: Jesus!), the more you can be happy when others get something good too. Because when it comes down to it, it's really not that much fun being jealous. It's a whole lot more fun just being you.

Who have you been jealous of lately? Have you said or done anything that might have accidentally hurt them? Maybe you could go to them and apologize, or do something nice for them. You never know when that kindness might come back to you.

Life's Bus Stop

I remain confident of This: I will see The goodness of The Lord in The Land of The Living. Wait for The Lord; be strong and Take heart and wait for The Lord.

PSALM 27:13-14

Waiting at the bus stop. Waiting in line at the store. Waiting for your parents to pick you up from your friend's house. It might feel like some days you're always waiting. It isn't easy—in fact most of the time, it's boring.

Life is full of waiting, but the waiting that's especially hard is when it feels like God doesn't even notice you're waiting. Maybe there's something you've been asking him about for a long time, and it just doesn't feel like it's happening any time soon. You might have told him about a friend who's sick, or your grades that won't come up (no matter how hard you study), or your parents who just won't stop fighting.

In the Bible, God answers prayers in one of three ways: sometimes he says yes, sometimes he says no, and sometimes he says wait. You won't hear him say those words out loud, and that's what makes waiting so hard—trusting that he hears your prayer. But he promises he does, and he will be by your side until the waiting is over.

List one thing you're waiting for God to do in your life. Next to that write, "God is with me." You might not have an answer just yet, but he knows exactly what you need and will take care of you.

All That Glitters

[Aaron] took what they handed him and made it into an idol cast in the shape of a calf, fashioning it with a tool. Then they said, "These are your gods, Israel, who brought you up out of Egypt."

EXODUS 32:4

It might sound a little silly that the people God loved chose to worship a golden calf. A baby cow! These people knew the God of the universe—the one who had rescued them from their enemies—but they chose to worship something they made with their own hands. They were distracted from what really mattered; distracted by something that glittered but had no power.

It's easy to wonder how an entire group of people could worship something so fragile, but the truth is, it's easy for us to be distracted by things that glitter and shine too. It might be name-brand clothes, your parents' new car, or it might be anything that comes wrapped up underneath the Christmas tree. Of course, we don't bow down to these things, but sometimes it's easy to focus on them more than we should. You see, worship is when we give more worth to anything—an object, a person, or a place—than we do to God. He is the only one who deserves our worship and admiration.

Is there anything in your life that feels more important to you than God right now? (That's normal—we all struggle with learning to balance what's most important in life.) Can you tell God about that thing and ask him to help you worship him most?

Don't Run the Red Light

If we confess our sins, he is faithful and just and will forgive us our sins and purify us from all unrighteousness.

I JOHN 1:9

Have you ever done anything that made you feel really guilty later? Maybe it was cheating on a test, telling a lie, or fighting with your mom or dad. You might have lain awake in bed that night, your stomach turning, your mind replaying the situation over and over again.

That guilty feeling is actually a really good thing that God put inside of us to let us know we're in a danger zone. Guilt acts like a red light or a stop sign, and we don't want to rush right past the guilty feeling because we could get hurt. Guilt is shouting to us, "Stop! Rethink this! Something bad is going to happen!"

You can be sure you aren't the first person to feel guilt. The good news is, we can choose to do the right thing again. God promises that when that guilty feeling hits, he's there, ready to forgive if we'll just ask him. Then he'll give us the power to apologize and do what's right!

Is there anything you need to ask God's forgiveness for? Is there anything you need to ask someone else's forgiveness for? Make a note for yourself, and remember to make that situation right again. God is always waiting for us with forgiveness and open arms.

But I'm Not a Preacher

He said to them, "Go into all the world and preach the gospel to all creation."

MARK 16:15

You don't have to be a preacher, a priest, or a minister to share your faith with others. You don't have to stand on a street corner with a sign in your hand, practice your best radio announcer voice, or bang your Bible on the lunchroom table (in fact, let's definitely not bang that Bible). Sharing your faith can be easy, and the more you practice doing it, the easier it will be.

Don't get me wrong—telling your friends about your belief in God could be a little scary at first. The good news is, you can start just by being you—kind, thoughtful, and considerate. When you choose not to gossip, that's sharing your faith. When you choose to stand up for someone who's being bullied, that's sharing your faith. When you tell a friend you'll be praying for him, that's sharing your faith. The more kind things you do, the more people will ask you what's different about you. Then you can be ready with the answer that Jesus gives you power to do these things, and he'd like to do that for them too.

Is there someone you can share your faith with today? Write down one small action you can take to love someone else. Then don't leave it on paper. Get out there and do it!

Safe in the Cave

From The ends of The earTh I caLL To you, I caLL as my heart
grows faint; Lead me To The rock ThaT is higher Than I.
PSALM 61:2

Anxiety is a familiar feeling—your heart pounds and your hands tremble. Maybe your armpits start to sweat but you try your best to hide it because you don't want anyone to know what you're feeling. Feeling nervous happens to everyone, but it can be an embarrassing emotion that sometimes takes control of our bodies.

It's normal to be anxious about things like tests, doctor's visits, or confrontations with bullies at school. Maybe you're nervous about the big game, or even about just making the team. What do you do when your anxiety feels like it's taking control? David, in the Bible, prayed that God would take him to the rock that was taller than David was. He wasn't talking about an actual rock—he was talking about God, strong like a rock—over him in heaven, protecting him from all the anxiety he was feeling. God wants to be your rock too. Will you let him be that for you today?

Next time you feel anxious or scared, find a quiet place and close your eyes. Imagine yourself sitting just inside a cave—a strong rock—a place where no outside storm can hurt you. And if you're still feeling anxious, it's always a good idea to talk with someone you can trust to help you work it out.

Anchors Away!

We have this hope as an anchor for the soul, firm and secure.
It enters the inner sanctuary behind the curtain where our
forerunner, Jesus, has entered on our behalf.

HEBREWS 6:19–20A

Hope is a funny word. We say we hope there's no pop-quiz at school tomorrow, we hope it doesn't rain during the baseball game, or we hope that the guy or girl we have a crush on has a crush on us too. But the word "hope" can have a deeper meaning too.

The Bible says that Jesus is our hope—he is the only one who can bring us life that lasts forever. When we believe that he died on the cross to forgive the wrong things we've all done (and then he came back to life to conquer death!), we have the hope of going to heaven someday. That means that no matter what happens in this life, and no matter how tough things get sometimes, we have hope for the future—a future in heaven with Jesus and all of those who love him. This hope is strong and secure like an anchor, holding us firm even in the middle of life's difficult times. It's something we can count on—something that will never change. And that's something to be excited about!

Have you ever told Jesus that you believe in him and you want him to be in charge of your life? If not, can you do that today? If you have done that already, can you tell a friend about what Jesus has done for you?

I Want More!

May God give you heaven's dew and earth's richness.

GENESIS 27:28A

God wants to bless you. Yes, you. Maybe your life doesn't feel that way right now—you might not have the nicest clothes or the biggest house. People might judge you because your shoes aren't new or your haircut didn't turn out the way you'd hoped.

While sometimes God does bless us with possessions (earth's richness), other times he chooses to simply bless us with himself (heaven's dew). This means no matter how much or how little stuff we have, we have the most important thing of all—Jesus. He's with us when we're up, and he's with us when we're down. He's with us when we're hungry, and he's with us when we have full bellies. He's with us when we win, and when we lose. There's no person in the whole world who can be there for us like Jesus, and the Bible says he's a friend who sticks closer than a brother. That's the greatest blessing of all.

Do you ever struggle with wanting more possessions, more things? Can you thank Jesus today, for the gift of himself?

I Don't Like Her

"In the beginning God created the heavens and the earth."
GENESIS 1:1

From the beginning of time God knew your name. When he spun the planets into space and set the sun high in the sky, he was already thinking about you. Your thumbprints, your personality, your DNA—all of these make you uniquely gifted to change this great big world.

Sometimes, though, it might not feel like you have any power to change anything. After all, you might not get to decide what time you get up, where you go to school, or even what cereal's in your bowl for breakfast.

There is one thing you always get to decide, though: how you treat others. Will you show the same appreciation that God showed when he created you? That person you meet today— the one you don't like so much—she was thought out by God before there was time or space. The creator of the universe thought of her eye color, hair color, and even her body type. You might not get along with her, but she is still God's unique creation—and that's something you can respect.

Go outside and breathe in the cool air God created. Say a prayer for someone you don't like very much. Ask God for his power to love that person—after all, he made the universe and his power lives in you.

33

No One Understands

Cast your cares on The Lord and he will sustain you; he will never let The righteous be shaken.

PSALM 55:22

Have you ever felt lonely, like no one else in the whole world can understand what's going on with you? Maybe your family doesn't treat you fairly, or friends at school make fun of you. Sometimes no matter how hard we try we just can't seem to make things better.

Can I tell you a secret? God sees you and he hears your prayers. Even though you can't feel or see him, he is with you always. He also knows what it's like to live in a human body and feel disappointed too. He walked this earth, and he knows exactly how it feels to be treated unfairly or to feel sad. The Bible says when you ask him to take your pain, he's waiting to help you feel better.

Write down what's bothering you today. You might even be able to start a specific notebook to write down the things that annoy or bother you, or about the times no one else seems to understand. When you're worried or alone, write these words: "God will never leave me." It's true.

Cleaning House

Do not judge, and you will not be judged. Do not condemn, and you will not be condemned. Forgive, and you will be forgiven.
LUKE 6:37

Have you ever felt judged by someone else? Maybe it was because of something you said, did, or even something as crazy as who you hung out with. It never feels great to be judged, does it?

How do you think other people feel when we judge them? We might think if we don't tell the other person that we're judging them, we're not hurting anyone. The truth is, we're actually hurting ourselves even when we quietly judge. Sometimes when we're criticizing someone else, it's so we can make ourselves feel better about who we are (even if we don't realize it).

But God says we have no right to judge anyone—he made that person, he called them special, and he is the only one who can judge them. When we choose to not judge, it frees us from all of the bad feelings we have about that person. It's a little like cleaning your room: suddenly you have a ton of space for all the things you really love and want to spend time on.

Would you let God change your heart today? Say this prayer: God, I choose to not judge ____. I ask you to help me be free from all the bad feelings I have about him so I can focus on loving others like you do. In Jesus' name, amen.

Not in the Principal's Office

Get wisdom, get understanding; do not forget my words or turn
away from them. Do not forsake wisdom, and she will protect
you; love her, and she will watch over you.
PROVERBS 4:5-6

D id you know wisdom can be like a good friend? When you spend a lot
of time learning about your friend, Wisdom, she will hang out with you
and help you make good decisions. Where can you find Wisdom, though?
Is she standing at the bus stop? Hanging out at your school (definitely not
in the principal's office)? Sitting at the cool table at lunch? Maybe, maybe
not, but the best place to find Wisdom is in the Bible. The more you read,
the more you know—and the more you know, the more you can practice
how to be smart in every situation in your life.

Gaining wisdom is a great adventure you get to take. Every person in
history, who ever made a good impact on the world, practiced wisdom. So
next time you're faced with a big decision, check out your devotional or
ask someone you trust about what's going on in your life. (Did you know
there's a whole list in the back of this book that tells you which page can
answer which life question? Really!) Choose to make the wise decision,
because in the end, that decision could change everything.

How can you make a wise decision today? Wisdom is something that
needs to be practiced, and the more you practice something the better
you get at it. What's one choice you can make today that will be a wise one?

You're in His "In Crowd"

See what great Love The Father has Lavished on us, That we
should be called children of God! And That is what we are!

I JOHN 3:1a

Is the popular crowd at your school really small? Are you a part of it, or do you find yourself sitting far away, with a totally different group of people? No matter where you sit, God sees you. No matter who you hang out with, God thinks you're awesome.

A lot of people in the world might want to change you. They might want you to wear different clothes, get a different hair-style, or take part in some crazy stuff just so you can fit in. But do you know where you will always fit in? With God. The Bible says you are his kid. He will defend you, love you, and fight for you. So no matter how popular or unpopular you might feel, keep being the real you. Whether that's athletic, the life of the party, or quiet and thoughtful, there is only one person who can be the amazing you. And that's the person God created and loves.

Are you feeling like yourself today, or do you feel like you have to hide who you are to fit in? Write down some things that might describe the "real you"—the person that no one else can see. Now write down one or two steps you can take (i.e., learn an instrument or practice football) to grow into that person you really are.

DAY 31

Sticking Like Glue

A friend loves at all times, and a brother is born for a time of adversity.

PROVERBS 17:17

What do you do when someone you care about is being made fun of? Maybe you used to hang out all the time with that friend, but you're afraid of being made fun of too. It would be really easy to walk away or ignore what's happening. The truth is, though, your friend needs you more than ever.

Imagine you're the one being picked on. The teasing and the bullying feel like too much to take, and no one's standing up for you. It's like they don't even see it's happening, or maybe your "friends" even join in just because everyone else is doing it. How would you feel?

Sticking by a friend who's having a hard time is called *loyalty*, and it's something the Bible talks about a lot. God is always loyal to you even when things are tough—and he wants to give you the power to be loyal for your friend.

Close your eyes and imagine yourself being strong for your friend. Ask God to give you the courage to be loyal to your friend, even if it's hard to do. You can do it!

But I Hate It

Do everything without grumbling or arguing, so that you
may become blameless and pure.

PHILIPPIANS 2:14–15A

Do you have to feed the dog? Make your bed? Scrub the toilet every single Saturday? Maybe you don't do chores, but you sure hate getting up for school every day. You might even hate waiting at the bus stop or doing your homework.

It's easy to complain about the stuff we don't like doing. Did you know God says that doing hard or even boring stuff makes us stronger? It does! It's like running—the more you do it, the stronger your legs and lungs will get. Your legs won't get strong by not complaining about chores, but your attitude will. You'll find yourself a little happier and a little more energetic to finish your job quickly and move on to what you really want to do.

So next time you're tempted to complain, remember: God rewards the faithful. He has big stuff in store for you when you practice not complaining!

Make a list of the things you dislike doing. Pick one and next time you're tempted to complain about it, practice telling God you're thankful for making you stronger.

Did You Hear What She Said?

Do not let any unwholesome talk come out of your mouths, but only what is helpful for building others up according to their needs, that it may benefit those who listen.

EPHESIANS 4:29

Sometimes it's spoken in a whisper—sometimes it's spoken in a loud voice in the locker room. Gossip is not a new phenomenon, because hey, it's always been entertaining to talk about someone else's problems. Gossiping also might make you feel better about your life for one minute when you point out how much worse someone else's is (until the guilt starts in).

Tough stuff happens: boyfriends and girlfriends break up, friends get failing grades, and classmates get cut from teams. How do you think those people feel when they find out we talk about them behind their backs? Are they angry? Do they want to hide under the covers and skip class because they're embarrassed? Do they want to lash out by talking bad about us?

The Bible says life and death are in the power of the tongue. That means you have the power to choose life for someone, to build them up and say nice things. It might mean feeling a little awkward by not saying anything when others gossip, or by walking away. But in the end, it's what you hope someone else would do for you.

Make a promise to yourself that next time someone talks badly about someone else, you'll choose to stand up for that person. Then pray and ask God for the strength to follow through on that promise.

Even When It Hurts

May The God of hope fill you with all joy and peace as you Trust in him, so That you may overflow with hope by The power of The Holy Spirit.

ROMANS 15:13

What makes you really happy? Is it hanging out with your best friend? Watching your favorite TV show? Playing your favorite sport? What would you do if you couldn't do that thing anymore?

When something important to us is taken away, we may feel sad or even angry. Sometimes things don't turn out the way we want them to, but God says even when we feel disappointed, he can give us joy.

Joy doesn't mean we have to pretend we don't have sad feelings about what happened, it just means we can practice being thankful for what we have: Jesus. Our friendship with Jesus is something that can never be taken away, even when other things we care about change. When we practice being thankful, we can get through the hard times and even learn from them.

What are you thankful for today? Even if you're feeling upset about a change in your life, can you tell Jesus what you're grateful for? That joy will make a difference for you.

The Web

Keep your Tongue from evil and your Lips from Telling Lies.
PSALM 34:13

You had just one second to make a decision, and you didn't make the best one. You might have chosen to take a peek at the test on the desk next to you. You might have chosen to pick up the candy bar in the check-out lane without paying for it. You might have chosen to tell your mom you lost your report card when you know exactly where it is. Now someone's asking you to tell the truth about what happened—and you're feeling a little stuck.

Sometimes telling the truth is hard to do. But the thing about telling a lie is that it's like spinning a great big spider web—you have to keep telling more lies to cover up the first lie, and pretty soon you've spun such a tale that you get caught right in the middle. Wouldn't you rather just tell the truth so that others know they can trust you to own up to your mistakes? Be a person who's known for telling the truth, even when it's tough.

Is there a lie you need to own up to? Can you ask God's forgiveness, and the forgiveness of the person you lied to? Don't put it off—do it today!

What Does He Call You?

... And he will be called Wonderful Counselor, Mighty God, Everlasting Father, Prince of Peace.

ISAIAH 9:6B

When you were born, your family gave you a name. Maybe it was Mark, or Jake, or Zoe. There are a million names in the world, but when God names a person, he gives that name meaning.

Do you know what God calls you? If you know Jesus as your savior, he calls you his child. That means you belong to him—no takebacks, no returns. You might have a great earthly father, or you might not know who your father is. The really cool thing is that no matter what your biological father is like, God your Father will never fail you. He will be your wonderful counselor, your strong God, and the one who gives you peace—no matter what your day has been like or how tough things get.

When you're feeling sad or alone, remember that your Father is there He wants to be your safe place—the one you can tell anything to. He'll always keep your secrets and always be there when you cry, or celebrate with you when things go your way.

Thank you, God, for being my Father. Thank you for being there at the low times and the high times. Thank you for being with me right now, cheering me on. I love you.

What's in the Box?

Gracious words are a honeycomb, sweet to the soul and healing to the bones.

PROVERBS 16:24

A delivery person comes to your door, and he or she brings a big package. Maybe what's inside is a mystery—maybe it's marked with a special word: FRAGILE. That word means that something delicate is in there and will shatter easily: Be warned, you need to be gentle with it!

In life, people are a lot like the packages you get on your doorstep. We can only see the outside, and even though people seem like they're doing okay, you never know what they're feeling inside. Maybe your best friend puts on a happy smile, but you don't know that he's listening to his parents argue every single night as he's trying to fall asleep. He might feel fragile inside, and you need to treat him gently—with kindness.

Other people are difficult to treat gently—they're rough on the outside and unkind to everyone around them. Those people especially need to be treated with kindness. There's probably a reason they're feeling sad and angry. Maybe you think they don't deserve niceness, but Jesus treats us kindly even when we don't deserve it. Who can you treat gently today?

Write down names of some people you know who might need kindness. What's one small way you can show that gentleness to them?

Are You Listening?

If anyone, Then, knows The good They oughT To do and doesn'T do iT, iT is sin for Them.

JAMES 4:17

Does your mom ever call you to come inside but you pretend not to hear? Maybe you get a text that says, "Come home," but you're having too much fun at your friend's house. Or maybe your dad says to clean the dust bunnies from under your bed, but you turn on the TV instead (after all, it's time for your favorite show).

There are a lot of ways to procrastinate. You can say, "Oh, I have to go to the bathroom!" or "My stomach really hurts," or "I just don't feel like it." But by putting off doing what you know is right, you're only punishing yourself! If you get your homework done right away, you have tons of free time to hang out with your friends. Plus, when you do the right thing right away, your responsibilities aren't hanging over your head when you're trying to have fun.

Give it a try today! Take the initiative to get things done and see how great it feels.

Get organized! Make a list of your responsibilities for today then give yourself a deadline to accomplish them. Don't try to take on too much too fast, though—pace yourself and you'll have time for work and fun.

The Last Slice of Pizza

Finally, all of you, be like-minded, be sympathetic, love one another, be compassionate and humble.

1 Peter 3:8

You're sitting in the car and your brother and sister are arguing (or maybe it's your parents). Is the argument about who gets the last slice of pizza, or who gets to use the computer first when you get home? Maybe it isn't just your brother and sister arguing—maybe you're arguing too.

Sometimes life isn't fair. You have to stand up for yourself when no one else will. But do you find yourself shouting a lot? Are you always the one coming in first place? Or are you sometimes willing to give up that last good thing in the fridge?

The Bible says when you put others first, you'll be blessed. You don't always have to be the one to get all the good stuff—sometimes you can take joy just knowing that someone else is getting happiness from something you gave up. Try it today: see if you can put someone else first. You might be surprised at how good it makes you feel!

Dear God, help me to be a cheerful giver today. Help me to be happy even when I don't get all the best stuff. Help me to live like Jesus—with a heart that is kind and wants good for others too. In Jesus' name, amen.

Hotheaded

A genTLe answer Turns away wrath, buT a harsh word
STirs up anger.

PROVERBS 15:1

What happens when you get angry? Do you start to sweat? Does your face get hot? Do your hands start to shake? Sometimes when we're mad, words come pouring out of our mouths that we know we shouldn't say. We want that other person to know exactly how we feel, even if it hurts them (in fact, we might be so angry that we hope our words do hurt).

We almost always regret what we say when we are angry. But there is another way—a way we can keep ourselves from having to live with the sadness of hurting someone.

We can walk away in the middle of an argument and say, "Excuse me for a minute." We can find a safe place, take some deep breaths, and ask for God's help to be kind. When we find our calm again, we can use the "soft answer" the Bible talks about—the gentle words we need to sort out the argument. When we use kindness, we help our bodies and minds stay healthy, and we help others learn kindness too.

Can you practice giving a kind answer to someone who wants to argue with you? Next time your classmate or sibling makes you angry, practice walking away and calming down before you talk.

A Few of Your Favorite Things

John answered, "Anyone who has two shirts should
share with the one who has none, and anyone who has
food should do the same."

LUKE 3:11

What's your most prized possession? Do you hide it when friends come
over because you're afraid someone might break it? Or do you bring
it out because you want to show everyone how cool it is? What if someone
asked if they could borrow your favorite thing?

It might be a skateboard, a book, or a DVD, but whatever it is, it's
hard to share something that means so much to you. Of
course, you don't have to let your friend use it—but when
you do choose to share (if you know they take good care
of things), you're doing what God's done for you.

He shared eternal life! That means life that lasts forever
in heaven. One day you can go to heaven if you trust him to
forgive the wrong things you've done. He set the example by
sharing an amazing gift with us—what can you share today?

Can you thank God today for sharing eternal life with you?
When you're done thanking him, can you think of someone you can share
with? Your sharing might even mean sharing the good news about Jesus
with someone you love!

Street Hockey

Likewise, The Tongue is a small part of The body, but iT makes great boasts. Consider whaT a greaT foresT is seT on fire by a small spark.

JAMES 3:5

Have you ever been in the grocery store with your mom and you are soooo bored? The cart is so full it should take a superhero to move it—but somehow your mom is still shopping. To top it off, you're pretty sure your friends are playing street hockey outside your house . . . without you.

What do you do? It seems reasonable at this moment to remind your mom for the fourteenth time that you'd like to go home to grab your gear. But she already has that grimace on her face that says you're grounded for life if you open your mouth.

Did you know situations like this are great times to practice self-control? The Bible says the most difficult part of your body to control is your tongue. It's hard not to use your mouth to whine at your parents, eat the last three cookies, or gossip about someone at school. But the cool thing about self-control is that the more you practice it, the better you get at it. And the better you get at it, the more like Jesus you'll be.

Dear Jesus, will you help me practice self-control? I can't do it on my own, but I know with your help I can grow into being the mature person you want me to be. Amen.

DAY 43

You Lost

The Lord is close to the brokenhearted and saves those who are crushed in spirit.

PSALM 34:18

Have you ever lost something you cared a lot about? Maybe it was your homework (uh-oh—teacher problems) or your favorite watch. Maybe you lost the whole wad of Christmas cash your grandma gave you, and you can't buy that one thing you've been saving for.

There's a different kind of loss the Psalms talk about—it's when someone we love dies and goes to heaven. It's one of the most painful losses we can experience, and it's really hard to know what to say when a friend loses a loved one.

You can have empathy. That means you can love your friend just by letting yourself feel their sadness. Put yourself in their shoes and imagine how brokenhearted they must feel. You don't always need to say something to make it better—just being there and offering hugs might be all your friend needs. It doesn't take much to show empathy, but it could make a huge difference in your friend's life.

Are you ready to show empathy to someone who's hurting? Next time someone you know loses a friend or a pet, be ready with a hug and an understanding heart.

Do You Have an Enemy?

My help comes from The Lord, The Maker of heaven and earth.
PSALM 121:2

If your teacher asked your class if they had an enemy, how many hands would pop into the air? Probably every single one! That enemy might be an old friend, an unkind teammate, or a bully at school.

Enemies don't always have to be people. Sometimes the enemy is a difficult problem, like a tough subject in school. It could be that mountain your summer camp counselor wants to you climb, or the mountain of dishes in the sink you're supposed to wash (yuck).

The Bible is full of stories of good people who faced tough enemies—there was even a young man named David who took on a giant and won. That doesn't mean you have to tackle your enemy at the bus stop, but it does mean Jesus is with you when things are tough. If you're being bullied you should ask an adult for help. If you're struggling with your grades you could find a quiet place to study (or see if someone can tutor you). There are a lot of ways to face the enemies in your life, but always remember God can help you when you're going through a hard time.

Thank you, Jesus, that you're with me when I'm having a tough time. Thank you that I can trust you to never leave me. Amen.

Looking Good

For we are God's handiwork, created in Christ Jesus to do good works, which God prepared in advance for us to do.

EPHESIANS 2:10

Have you ever heard the saying, "Pretty is as pretty does"? People can be pretty on the outside, but if they aren't pretty on the inside—if they don't do things that are kind and right—well, they really aren't all that beautiful.

God says he created you—yes, you—as his handiwork (you look good!). You are his art project. Every detail was carved by his hands, and from the shape of your nose to the length of your spine, he paid close attention to making you the perfect you. Whether you're too short to reach the countertop or so tall you can reach the top of the basketball hoop, you're exactly the way God wanted.

Most importantly, he planned for you to do great things for others—to do beautiful deeds—before you were even born! One of those great adventures is loving many different kinds of people along the way. So what will you do next time someone different comes along? Remember: good-looking is as good-looking does!

Write down some ways you can care for others who are different than you, especially if others give that person a hard time. Ask God to give you the courage to be kind.

Jumping from the Plane

And I pray That you, being rooted and established in Love, may have The power, TogeTher wiTh aLL The Lord's holy peopLe, To grasp how wide and Long and high and deep is The Love of ChrisT.

EPHESIANS 3:17B–18

Have you ever watched a stunt person jump from an airplane? The airplane is so high, hovering overhead, when all of the sudden a tiny black speck comes tumbling out towards the ground. A parachute opens like a giant mushroom, bringing the person safely down to the ground.

That airplane was probably speeding along at about 12,000 feet above the earth—but it wasn't anywhere near how far a space shuttle blasts into orbit. Can you imagine—God's love for you goes even higher and wider and deeper than the entire universe that he created? The galaxies we haven't even discovered yet can't even contain his affection for you.

So next time you're feeling a little lonely or wondering if God's on your side—know that he is. With his love behind you, you have all the love you need to share on this adventure called life.

How can you share God's love today? Maybe you could do the dishes for your mom or take out the trash for your grandpa. God's love is so huge it isn't meant to be kept to yourself—share it with someone!

Future President?

Seek The Lord, all you humble of The Land, you who do what he commands.

ZEPHANIAH 2:3A

What do you do if you want to be president? You get on television, travel the country, and tell everyone why you're the right person for the job. It's the same in almost every leadership competition: you tell everyone why you're the best choice.

Being a leader in God's family is the opposite. If you want to lead people for God, the Bible says over and over again that you have to be humble— willing to put others before yourself. It's kind of like being the person on an airplane who sits by the emergency exit: you have to be willing to go last if there's a problem, and you may even suffer because of it.

What place do you have in God's family? Whether or not you want to be a leader, remember to treat others better than yourself, put others first, and be like Jesus—the one who gave everything for us.

Dear Jesus, I want to love others the way you do. Help me to put others first because I love you, not because I want others to like me. In Jesus' name, amen.

Bad News

Peace I leave with you; my peace I give you. I do not give
to you as the world gives. Do not let your hearts be
troubled and do not be afraid.

JOHN 14:27

Do you ever watch the news with your parents or listen to it on the radio? Sometimes what's happening in the world might seem scary or sad. Sometimes what's happening in your own life might feel scary or sad too.

Jesus says he wants to give you peace. Peace means that no matter what's happening in your life, you know Jesus is taking care of you. (When you're on an adventure, there's going to be some scary stuff sometimes!)

Is someone you love sick? Did your best friend move? Is there drama in the locker room? All of these things can sneak in like a thief and steal your peace. It's hard to know how to get it back, but Jesus says he's the prince of peace—that means he has all the comfort you need. By stepping away into a quiet place for a few minutes, you can get away from your problem and ask Jesus to give you his peace again. He's waiting right there to give it to you.

Remember, Jesus is taking care of you. Write down what's stealing your peace. Now write down something you can do to find that peace again.

The Power to Do What's Right

Do you not know that your bodies are temples of the Holy Spirit, who is in you, whom you have received from God? You are not your own; you were bought at a price. Therefore honor God with your bodies.

I CORINTHIANS 6:19–20

Did you know that no one had to teach you how to tell a lie? No one had to teach you how to shout angry words. And no one had to teach you how to cheat on a test—your eyes already knew how to wander to look at someone else's page.

You and everyone in the world were born knowing how to sin. But when you gave your life to Jesus, he came to be with you. Your body belongs to him now, and he wants to help you do the right thing with it.

What should you do when you're tempted to lie, scream, or cheat on a test? You can remember that Jesus lives in you and gives you the power to do what's right. He promises that when you ask him to help you honor him with your body, he'll be right there—helping you do what's right.

What's the one thing you struggle with most? Is it fighting? Lying? Gossiping? Can you write that one thing down, then write: "My body belongs to Jesus. He can help me overcome this!"

A Night at the Movies

Follow my example, as I follow the example of Christ.

I Corinthians 11:1

Do you like to watch a good movie? Action and adventure? Comedy? Who's your favorite actor or actress? It's fun to keep up with your favorite stars. You might get on their websites or follow them on social media. You might even read their advice or imitate how they dress.

Did you know most movie stars are just normal people like you? They get up in the morning and put their pants on one leg at a time. They eat and drink and they plan their days. They just sometimes have a camera in front of them while they do it (and probably a little more money in their pockets)! Sometimes movie stars don't make the best choices and don't live their lives by what God says is right and good, but sometimes we don't either.

We have to be careful not to take peoples' advice or copy how they live just because they are popular. In fact, the best place to get our advice is from people who know how we live—people who love Jesus and have been around longer than we have.

So go ahead! Have fun with those movies and TV shows. But remember—parents, grandparents, and church leaders might be the better place to go for advice.

Think about whom you admire. Can that person help you grow up to be more like Jesus? If not, then think about someone else you can go to for help!

DAY 51

Picking Teams

So in everything, do to others what you would have them do to
you, for this sums up the Law and the Prophets.

MATTHEW 7:12

You're standing in gym class and it's time to pick teams. Maybe you're the captain. Or maybe you're standing on the sidelines, waiting for your name to be called. Some of your friends look confident that they'll be picked right away—others look worried. Maybe you're shaking in your tennis shoes too.

It's no fun to be picked last. When you're the one doing the picking, your friends might get mad if you pick someone who isn't as fast or as good first. But it's important to think about how you would feel—whether picking a teammate or picking a study partner. There might be someone hoping you'll ask them to sit at your table at lunch. Maybe it's the new kid, and it's been so long since you were new, you've forgotten just how discouraging that can feel.

Can you pick someone different today? God says that when you do something for someone else you're following all of what the Bible says. It's what's most important, and the choice is yours today.

Who can you pick? Can you write their names down? Maybe you can start by simply sitting next to them on the bus or inviting them over after school.

A Voice in the Dark

Then Samuel said, "Speak, for your servant is listening."
I Samuel 3:10b

Can you imagine lying in bed and hearing a strange voice calling your name? There's no one else in the house—maybe you watched too many creepy TV shows today? Or maybe you left the TV on? Yes, that's it . . . but wait. It's off.

In the Old Testament (first half of the Bible), God sometimes spoke to people with his voice. He doesn't do that so much anymore because we have his words written down in the Bible—so how do we know where to get his advice when we need it?

There are three ways God usually helps us with our problems these days: first, through his Word in the Bible. Its pages are full of solutions to our problems (and this devotional book helps you learn about those). Second, if you know Jesus as your savior, his spirit is with you. That means he has given you a conscience, something inside of you that tells you when you're doing right or wrong. Third, worshiping God at church and asking older Christians for advice helps you become strong in your faith.

If you're still not sure what to do, you can find a trusted friend or older Christian who can help you work through your problem. You're not alone, and God wants to help you with every tough situation.

Dear God, you're my advice giver, my counselor. Thank you for giving me all of these ways to help me work through my problems. Help me to make smart decisions today.

What's in That Window?

You, therefore, have no excuse, you who pass judgment
on someone else, for at whatever point you judge
another, you are condemning yourself, because you who
pass judgment do the same things.

ROMANS 2:1

Have you ever noticed that you can take one look at a person and decide who that person is? Are they athletic? Do they have expensive clothes? Do they buy lunch at school, or bring a peanut butter and pickle sandwich? Have you ever felt judged by someone else? Maybe people don't treat you well because they think that by simply looking at you or watching who you hang out with they know who you are. But looking at someone and judging who they are is like looking in a window and thinking you've seen the whole house.

It hurts when others judge you and don't want to understand who you really are. But God says they don't have the right to do that, and they're only judging themselves because they're no different than you. When it comes down to it, no matter the color of our eyes, skin, or clothes—we're all the same. Human, loved by God, and created for a very special purpose.

Dear Jesus, help me not to judge others by the outside. Help me to appreciate each and every person in my life for who you made them to be. In Jesus' name, amen.

DAY 54

Brains and Stuff

Whatever you do, work at it with all your heart, as working for the Lord, not for human masters.
COLOSSIANS 3:23

Who's the smart kid in your class? Is it you? Is it the girl sitting in the front row? Or maybe the guy next to you who would rather read books than hang out after school?

Sometimes it's not considered "cool" to be smart. You might get laughed at if you seem to know all the answers in class. Maybe it's even tempting to not study because you'd rather be known as the cool kid.

Guess what? You can be smart *and* cool. When you study and do your homework, you're thinking about your future and who you want to be some day. God put you on this earth so that you could use all of the abilities he gave you, including your brain. You can use your mind and your body to work for God's kingdom. Don't worry about what other people think—just be the best you that you can be and you will make a difference!

What's one thing you're not doing your best at right now? How can you improve? Make a list of three things you can do to work hard and dream big!

Foraging for Food

Similarly, anyone who competes as an athlete does not receive
The victor's crown except by competing according to the rules.
2 TIMOTHY 2:5

Have you ever had to go into the forest to look for food? Probably not, but when God first created people, there wasn't a grocery store just up the road—they had to search for berries, vegetables, and animals to eat every day. God made people with the ability to run far and fast so they could survive in a world where they had to hunt for what they needed. That nature is still in you today because of how God created you—you're not competing for food now, but you are competing in things like sports and spelling bees.

Competition is important because it helps us become the best we can be. But sometimes when we're feeling competitive, we forget that people are more important than always winning. Some people, even adults, get so caught up in winning that they break the rules or hurt peoples' feelings just to get the prize.

Next time you're playing a board game, sport, or even participating in a spelling bee—remember to compete the right way. Play by the rules. Treat your competitors with respect and kindness. You can be a winner in games and in friendships!

Write down two ways you can compete the right way next time you're in a game situation. Put that paper somewhere you can see it when the time comes!

Doughnut Competition

Let us not become weary in doing good, for at the proper time we will reap a harvest if we do not give up.

GALATIANS 6:9

If your school or neighborhood announced a doughnut eating competition, would you be all in? Would you practice? Would you give it your best?

Some things are easy to practice, but the harder stuff can slow us down. Being kind to others is one of those things that might be more difficult to practice in the beginning. When a friend's hurting, did you know you can work hard at doing something nice for that person? When someone you know needs food, did you know you can use that situation to practice giving sacrificially? Loving others is something you can train yourself to do. When you practice doing loving things, you can learn to not grow weary in doing good for others and for God.

What would you like to do well? Can you ask God to help you get there? You'll need his power to give you the patience and endurance to keep up the good work.

Dodgeball

He saved us, not because of righteous things we had done, but because of his mercy.

TITUS 3:5A

Gym class—you either love it or you hate it. Do you like ducking in dodgeball, or do you dread the moment the ball is going to slam into the side of your head? There are really important rules to the game, and one of the most important ones is that you can't cross the line when you're throwing the ball at the other team. If you cross, it's game over.

But what if you break the rules and your P.E. coach tells you that once—just this once—you don't have to sit out? That you don't have to pay the penalty for making the wrong move?

That's what God did for us, but it was a much bigger deal than a dodgeball game. He showed us something called mercy when he decided we didn't have to pay for the wrong things we do (Jesus chose to do that for us instead). Because of the mercy God shows us, we can show mercy to others. When someone does something that hurts us, we can choose to forgive them.

Dear Jesus, thank you for your mercy. Thank you for forgiving me and helping me forgive others—showing mercy to them—like you've done for me.

Who Turned Out the Lights?

This is the message we have heard from him and declare to you:
God is light; in him there is no darkness at all.

1 John 1:5

If you've ever been to the country at night, you know how dark it can get. There aren't any streetlights, stoplights, or house lights. Just you and the moon and stars. After a while your eyes adjust to the darkness and you can find your way around, but you still can't see as well as if you had a light.

Jesus says he's a light. You can't keep him in your back pocket like a flashlight, but if you know him as your savior, he will help you make good decisions. Because of Jesus, there is something inside of you that tells you when you need to be nice to someone, study harder for a test, or go to bed when your parents tell you to. That feeling, that light, comes from Jesus.

Jesus is also your light in hard times. He's there when you feel like no one else is. He promises he'll never leave you no matter what tough stuff is happening in your life. That's way better than any light on a dark night.

Turn the lights out in your room tonight. How dark is it? Wait a minute for your eyes to adjust . . . then turn the light on again. It's the same with Jesus—it's so much easier to see when you let him be your light.

No Skydiving Allowed

Don'T LeT anyone Look down on you because you are young, buT seT an example for The believers in speech, in conducT, in Love, in faiTh and in puriTy.

I TIMOTHY 4:12

There are some things you can't do yet—like drive a car, work on a construction site, or sky-dive. Those things would be dangerous for someone who's not an adult, and making your own decisions might seem like it's a long way off (it'll be here before you know it, though).

Some adults might act like there are other things you can't do—like making a difference for God. But the Bible says that your age doesn't matter: you can do awesome stuff!

What words can you speak today that will make someone feel loved? What gift can you give to a hurting friend? How can you spend your time helping others? It doesn't matter what anyone else says, your age really doesn't matter when it comes to serving God. He has a big adventure planned for you, and this is only the beginning.

Jesus, with you I can make a difference. Help me to not be afraid of what other people think, and do big things for you anyway. Thank you for taking me on this adventure with you!

DAY 60

Follow the Leader

IT is The Lord your God you must follow, and him you must revere.
Keep his commands and obey him; serve him and hold fast to him.
DEUTERONOMY 13:4

Have you ever played follow the leader? When you were younger you probably played it with your friends, but now that you're older you might be playing the same game in everyday life without even realizing it. For instance, are you checking out what your friends are wearing and shopping for something similar? What about their attitudes—do you treat teachers and people in authority the same way your friends do, even when it's disrespectful?

God says that he's our leader. He sees the whole world and knows exactly how everything works. He gives us directions for a reason—to keep us safe and help us live long, happy lives. He wants us to do the right thing, even if doing what's right isn't always easy or cool.

So next time you're tempted to do what your friends are doing just to fit in, remember to ask yourself what Jesus would do. Is it the same as what your friends are doing? You can count on him to help you make smart decisions.

What's one way you can follow Jesus today? Maybe it means obeying the people who are in charge, or choosing not to do something dangerous your friends are doing. Ask God for the power to follow him today!

Awake Beside the Sheep

I am The good shepherd. The good shepherd Lays down his Life for
The sheep.

JOHN 10:11

Have you ever stayed overnight away from your home and family? Maybe you slept at a friend's house or you went to summer camp. Did you sleep indoors or did you sleep underneath the starry sky?

Camping outside can be fun but you might get tired of it after a while. Shepherds sleep outside with their sheep every night. Their job is to protect those big fluffy animals from wolves or anything that might try to harm them.

Jesus says he's your shepherd. He's watching out for you even when you're sleeping. He's there day and night. He likes being with you; it's not a job for him—he just enjoys being there. He not only wants to be with you when you sleep—he wants to guide you when you're awake. So if you're feeling a little lonely today, know that Jesus is with you. He's there to help you because he is your shepherd.

Thank you, Jesus, for being my shepherd. I trust you because you never sleep. Thank you for always being with me no matter what happens in this life.

DAY 62

Pinky Promise

ALL you need To say is simply 'yes' or 'No'; anything beyond This comes from The evil one.

MATTHEW 5:37

Have you ever had a friend tell you she'd do something with you then change her mind? It might have been something cool like going to the movies or it might have been something boring like helping with yard work. Maybe she didn't even have a good excuse—for whatever reason she just decided she didn't want to tag along.

God says following through on your promises is important. You can't make your friends follow through on their promises but you can follow through on yours. When you tell your mom you'll mow the lawn or your dad that you'll go to church, you should do it even when you don't feel like it.

An important part of keeping promises is deciding whether you really want to do something before you promise to do it. If you pause and think before you say yes to a friend or family member you'll keep yourself from making promises that are hard to keep. That way when you do what you promised others will know they can count on you.

Jesus, help me to keep my promises like you keep your promises to me. Is there anyone I should apologize to for breaking my word? Give me strength to do that today.

Life that Lasts

But whoever drinks the water I give them will never thirst. Indeed, the water I give them will become in them a spring of water welling up to eternal life.

JOHN 4:14

When was the last time you were super thirsty? Was there water nearby or did you have to wait for a drink? Wouldn't it be convenient if we could just carry a lifetime supply of water with us everywhere we go?

Jesus says he's like a big well that doesn't run dry. He won't cure your physical thirst, but he'll cure a much more important thirst—the thirst for everlasting life. Some people might think there are other ways to have everlasting life, but Jesus says he's the only way. Unlike the wells of water on earth that run dry, Jesus gives life that will never end. As you get older, people will try to convince you to try other wells (other religions or beliefs), but that's like drinking a hot beverage on a hot day—it's not the answer. Jesus is the only well that won't run dry, and he's the only one you can count on to give you life that lasts forever.

Jesus, I believe you're my well—that I need you more than I need water. You give me life that lasts forever!

Better than a Birthday

I will refresh The weary and saTisfy The faint.
JEREMIAH 31:25

When it's your birthday do you get really excited about presents? Do you beg your family for one thing in particular? Maybe you ask and ask and you're sure it's going to be the best thing ever. When you get your gift you're so excited you practically sleep with it next to you. Before you know it, though, the excitement wears off.

Scientists tell us that when we get something new that feeling of satisfaction lasts for about two weeks. Does that mean you should never ask for a special birthday present? Of course not! You just shouldn't expect that new thing to bring you satisfaction forever.

There is one thing—one person, actually—who can bring you forever satisfaction: Jesus. He says he's with you when everything else gets old, and he'll fill you up when you feel empty. Chasing after things will never make you truly happy because it wasn't designed to. Only God can do that!

God, thank you for all the good stuff you provide for me, but most of all thank you for giving me you. I'm sorry when I get distracted by all the stuff in my life. Help me to remember that only you satisfy!

Promising Yourself

BuT DanieL resoLved noT To defiLe himseLf wiTh The royaL food and wine, and he asked The chief officiaL for permission noT To defiLe himseLf This way.

DANIEL 1:8

The older you get the more you may notice there's a lot of temptation to do things that are wrong. Eventually someone might offer you drugs or try to get you to do stuff with your body that isn't okay if you're not married. It might feel exciting to know you're growing up, but it's important that you follow what the Bible and your parents say about your body and how to protect it.

One thing you can do to keep your body safe is exactly what Daniel did—he made a decision even before the temptation came that he wasn't going to harm himself. He "resolved" not to give into temptation—he was absolutely sure he was going to do the right thing. When you resolve beforehand not to do what non-Christians are doing, you don't have to depend on your emotions in the moment— you can depend on your mind to tell you to walk away.

You can be strong when temptation comes by deciding beforehand exactly what you'll do.

Think about something that people do that you're not supposed to. You could even write it down. Then write down your plan of action for when your moment of temptation comes.

A Surprise Ending

For what I received I passed on to you as of first importance:
That Christ died for our sins according to the Scriptures, that he
was buried, that he was raised on the third day according to the
Scriptures.

I CORINTHIANS 15:3–4

If you've ever been to a funeral you know just how sad it can be to lose someone you love. Jesus' friends lost someone they loved when he died on the cross. The Bible says they wept uncontrollably.

If you've experienced loss you probably miss your loved one a lot, and even though you have the hope of seeing them in heaven again, it's hard to wait. Jesus' friends thought they had no hope—they thought he was gone for good. Then in a surprise ending (even though he'd told them he was going to do this), Jesus came back to life three days after his death. No one in the world had ever overcome death like Jesus did—it was a spectacular ending to what seemed to be a sad story. Because of Jesus' resurrection we can trust him when he says he will bring everyone back to life one day. Heaven might feel far away right now, but we can look forward to a time when all God's family will be together again forever.

Thank you, Jesus, for dying for my sins and coming back to life. Thank you for overcoming death so that I can live with you forever.

He Never Sleeps

Indeed, he who watches over Israel will neither slumber nor sleep.

PSALM 121:4

When you stay over at a friend's do you stay up late into the night? Maybe you challenge each other to see how long you can keep your eyes open. Movies, snacks, and games—all these things can distract you from falling asleep. But no matter how hard you try you can't stay awake forever. Your body won't let you!

Did you know God never sleeps? He doesn't need to, and he especially never gets tired of hanging out with you. He's like a best friend at a slumber party—he wants to spend time with you and hear everything you're thinking. He has his eyes on you and everything that's happening in the world so you don't have to worry or be afraid. What's bothering you today? When you're in bed and your mind is racing and your eyes just won't close, remember he's hanging out with you and you can tell him anything. He'll take your worries and your fears so you can sleep safe and sound.

Dear God, you want to hang out with me. Even when I'm tired, you take my daily worries for me so I can sleep. I give those worries to you. Amen.

Obedience Looks Good on You

Listen, my son, to your father's instruction and do not forsake your mother's teaching. They are a garland to grace your head and a chain to adorn your neck.

PROVERBS 1:8-9

There's a secret rule written in the Bible that says, "Children, obey your parents—except when they're not looking." Wait a minute. Is that in the Bible? Some days it might seem a lot more convenient if that verse *was* in the Bible but it isn't—you're supposed to obey your parents even when they're not around.

Someone once said that "integrity" is doing what's right even when no one else is looking. Maybe that means that when you come home from school and want to watch TV you sit down at the kitchen table instead, and do your homework like your mom asked (all five pages of your essay!). The cool thing about obedience is that God says it looks good on you. When you obey with a good attitude it's like putting on your favorite T-shirt— it's cozy and comfortable because you know you're doing the right thing (even when it's hard). Obedience brings you success because when you respect authority God says he'll bless you with peace that you're doing the right thing.

Put on your favorite T-shirt and think about obedience. In which areas is it hard for you to obey your parents? What can you do to change that next time it comes up?

On Trend

We do not dare to classify or compare ourselves with some who commend themselves. When they measure themselves by themselves and compare themselves with themselves, they are not wise.

2 CORINTHIANS 10:12

How's it going on that bus ride to school? Who has the coolest cell phone? When you pause at the next stop who comes out of the biggest house? And what's going on with the cool kid whose hair is a different color every time you see him?

You don't have to ride the bus to school to notice that everyone has different stuff. You might look down at your own shoes and notice they're not the latest or greatest. It's hard to keep up with trends (it seems like they change every week) and comparing your stuff to other people's can leave you feeling empty or jealous. It's natural to compare what you have to what others have, but things are not what's important. What matters is how you treat others—not whether your clothes are trendy or whether you're just one style (or six) behind. Comparison steals your joy, but loving others is always in style. Next time you're tempted to compare yourself with the kid sitting next to you, do something nice for him instead.

Who did you compare yourself with today? Can you let that go and think of one kind act you can do for someone else? Soon you'll find your focus has changed from you, to giving someone else joy.

Stronger than a Castle

BuT The Lord is faithful, and he will strengthen you and protect
you from The evil one.

2 THESSALONIANS 3:3

Have you ever seen a picture of a castle or perhaps toured one? Some castles are old and run down, but some have walls that are still thick and strong—walls that protected people from the attack of their enemies.

It's important when you're being attacked to be able to find a safe place to hide—a place that's proven itself over time to be strong. God says that when hard times come, he wants to be your safe place. That means when there's nowhere else to go and no one else you can trust he'll take care of you. The Bible says God's like a strong tower you can run to when you're afraid. He's faithful—he'll never crumble and he'll never fail no matter how bad things get. He'll not only shelter you when you're worried, he'll strengthen you to stand up against whatever's attacking you. The best part is you don't even have to build your safe place. He's already there. All you have to do is ask for his help.

Dear God, you're better and stronger than any fort. I promise when I'm afraid I will pray to you. Thank you for being my faithful friend and the one who shelters me.

No Evil Thing

I wiLL noT Look wiTh approval on anyThing ThaT is vile.
PSALM 101:3A

Your parents aren't home and you know the password on the TV. Before you know it, you've unlocked an entire world of TV possibilities, and none of them involve the kids' channels.

Okay, so none of this happened to you—but it can be tempting when you're being a couch potato to let the remote stop on channels you know you shouldn't be watching. There's a big wide world of things you've never seen or heard, but those channels also come with dangers—not all knowledge is good knowledge, and not everything you see on TV is true. David wrote in the Psalms that he wouldn't look at anything that was evil. There's a reason for that: he knew that once he saw something bad he couldn't un-see it. It would be in his memory forever, and he wanted to think about only things that would please God.

What about you? Will you promise yourself today that you will put no evil thing in front of your eyes?

Think about the next time you feel tempted to watch or look at something you know isn't right. What will you do? The best plan you can make for yourself is to turn it off and distract yourself with a good book—like the Bible or this devotional. Tell an adult or a mentor what you're going through and they can help you learn how to resist temptation.

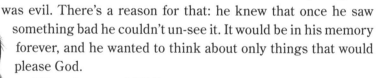

Don't Fall for Pride

Pride goes before destruction, a haughty spirit before a fall.
PROVERBS 16:18

From the time you're little, you're taught to be proud of the things you accomplish. When you score big on the field or earn an A in the classroom your parents and teachers probably say, "I'm proud of you!"

Why does the Bible say we shouldn't be proud then? It's actually telling you about a different type of pride—a pride that says, "I know everything. No one can teach me anything." This kind of pride makes others not want to be around you, because it's no fun listening to someone who brags. You were born to learn and you will keep learning for all your life. No matter how many touchdowns you score, there's always someone who can help you do better. You should respect your teachers and coaches because they've been around for a long time, and they know how to help you become the best person you can be. Choosing not to be proud means choosing to become the best person you can be.

Dear God, I'm sorry if I've been prideful or looked down on those around me. Help me remember that you're the one who gives me the ability to do everything—you're the one who gives me breath in my body. Help me to honor you with my attitude.

Bigger than the Storm

"Do not come any closer," God said. "Take off your sandals, for the place where you are standing is holy ground."
EXODUS 3:5

When a tornado hits, you take cover—probably in the deepest basement or ditch you can find. Storms are powerful and you know by instinct to respect them.

God's more powerful than a storm—he's the creator of all nature. Because we can't see or touch him, though, sometimes we forget just how powerful he is. We might talk a lot about his goodness and love, but what about his holiness and might? In the Old Testament, Moses was one of the few people who saw God's glory firsthand. When he met with God he was told to take off his shoes because the ground where he stood was holy. Removing his shoes was a sign of respect. We don't remove our shoes when we go to church, but we can show our respect in other ways. When the pastor or priest is speaking, we can pay attention and not text or pass notes. We can also listen and apply what we learn to our everyday lives. God is loving, but he is also holy. He deserves our respect.

Dear God, I praise you because you are holy. Thank you for loving me and wanting me to walk in your ways. Help me to respect you today.

Taking the Cookie

Woe To you, Teachers of The Law and Pharisees, you hypocrites!
You clean The outside of The cup and dish, but inside They are full
of greed and self-indulgence.

MATTHEW 23:25

Have you ever reached out to grab a chocolate chip cookie fresh out of the oven and gotten burned? You were in a hurry to get the good stuff but your rushing only got you hurt.

God brings us different blessings at different times in our lives. Sometimes, though, (like that chocolate chip cookie) we get in a hurry and start grabbing for what doesn't belong to us. It could be that you want to be class president, or you want to earn a lot of money or be the first in line at the movie theater. Those are all okay ambitions but how are you getting there? When you are in a hurry and lose sight of other people's feelings, it's called greed. Before you know it, you're hurting other people just to get what you want. It's never worth stepping on someone else's head just to get to the top. Make sure you think of others first and you'll be right on track.

The opposite of greed is sharing. What can you share today? Write it down and hold yourself to it when you're tempted to give into greed.

Faith for the Finish Line

Now faith is confidence in what we hope for and assurance about what we do not see.

HEBREWS 11:1

When you're running a race you join the group at the starting line. There's probably a huge crowd of people and it may make it hard to see what's ahead of you. The whistle sounds and it's time to go—everyone takes off as fast as they can in the same direction. You can't see the finish line, but you know it's there.

The Bible says life is a lot like a race. You're running toward Jesus and your heavenly home, but you can't see either one just yet. Sometimes it's hard to have faith that he's waiting at the end. Other people might stand on the sidelines and challenge you—they might try to bully you into doubting where you're going. But that's all they are: bullies. You're going to reach spots in the race when you think you can't finish. Life might seem too difficult and overwhelming. That's part of your amazing journey: it won't all be easy but you will make it. You can have faith that Jesus is cheering you on and waiting for you at the finish line.

What's worrying you today? What's making it hard to believe that Jesus cares? Can you write it down and ask him to help you have faith that he can help you through?

Live Free

Keep your servant also from willful sins; may they not rule over me. Then I will be blameless, innocent of great transgression.

PSALM 19:13

What would you do if someone stole your most treasured possession? Would you confront them? What if when you asked why they took the item the response was, "Because I wanted to." That person would be willfully doing what is wrong—intentionally hurting you. Sometimes we do the same thing to God; we choose our own way because we want to—it's not an accident.

Are there willful sins in your life right now? Are you choosing to be mean to the short kid on the bus? Mouthing off to your teacher? Refusing to do your homework? Anything you do that you know is wrong is willful sin. Willful sin not only hurts the people around you, it also hurts you. God says this type of wrongdoing is like a trap that grabs on and keeps you from a relationship with him. He wants to help you be free from willful sin so that it doesn't control you. What's holding you back today? Would you like to be free?

Dear God, I'm sorry for making the wrong choice by (*tell God your sin*). I don't want to live like this any longer. Help me make good choices and apologize to the people I've hurt because of my sin. Amen.

Not Just Your Best Friend

And if you greet only your own people, what are you doing more
than others? Do not even pagans do that?
MATTHEW 5:47

Do your best friends do nice things for you? Do they wait for you at the bus stop or walk to class with you? Do they remember your birthday and give you the perfect gift? Maybe they listen when you're down and stand up for you when others tease you.

It's easy to do nice things for people we like but what about the people we don't always like? The Bible says that even people who aren't Christians do nice things for their friends, so if we're only loving people who are nice back how are we different from non-Christians? What about that kid no one wants to hang out with? He's not your friend, but maybe you could invite him over to your table. And the girl who spreads gossip about you? Maybe you could meet her with a smile tomorrow morning. Think about things you would do for your best friends and try to do some of those things for others too. God loved us before we loved him back—he can help us love those who don't love us back.

Think of one person you can do something nice for today. Write down that one thing and follow through on it. You can make a difference by loving those who don't love you.

Alpha & Omega

"I am The Alpha and The Omega," says The Lord God, "who is, and who was, and who is To come, The Almighty."

REVELATION 1:8

Who was there when God spoke the world into existence? Who watched the first waves of the ocean and listened to the first cry of the animals? Who smelled the first breath of new fresh air? God was the only one watching, listening, and creating. The Bible says he has always been and always will be. Every page of history and every page of the future are his. We don't know what will happen, but God does.

He is the alpha and omega—these Greek letters mean he's the beginning and the end. God's the alpha and omega in your life too. He was there when you were born and he will be there the very last day of your life and beyond. He has a plan for every moment of your life. He's not too big to notice when you're sad and he's not too busy to notice when you're happy. He's on your side. You can always count on him to be there because he has been from the beginning of time.

What's making you happy today? What's making you sad? Can you tell God about it? He's always there, and he always will be.

Are You Holy?

Consecrate yourselves and be holy, because I am The Lord your God.
Keep my decrees and follow them. I am The Lord, who makes you holy.
LEVITICUS 20:7-8

Do you like fitting in? Have you noticed how easy it seems for the popular people? They might shop at the same stores, have the same phones, and wear the same styles. If you watch them walk into school they might look a little like clones of each other.

There's nothing wrong with wanting to belong, but there is one area where the Bible says we should be different: holiness. Not the kind of holy where you think you're better than someone else, but the kind of holy where you choose to do the right thing because God is holy. God made the choice to come to earth, even though it isn't a holy place. He was tempted to do the wrong things when he was here, but the Bible says he never thought, said, or did anything wrong.

You're not God, and you'll never achieve perfection. But he has set you apart—made you different from the world. Every day you can make choices that will help you be a little more like Jesus. What choices can you make today? You were made to stand out—you don't have to be a clone.

What's one thing you can do today to choose holiness? Ask God to give you the strength to live less like the world and more like him.

DAY 80

Bigger Than the Battle

This is what The Lord says to you: 'Do not be afraid or discouraged because of this vast army. For the battle is not yours, but God's.'
2 Chronicles 20:15b

Maybe you woke up this morning and pulled the covers back over your head. The light was shining through your window but there was something you were dreading—something about your day you just didn't want to face.

God knows that life gets hard sometimes. There are tough tests at school, tough people to deal with, and tough emotions to handle. Maybe you don't even tell your parents exactly how hard things get—it seems like there's no one you can talk to who will understand. Life wasn't meant to be easy, but it also wasn't meant to be done alone. God says whatever battle you're facing today, don't be discouraged. Your fight might seem bigger than you—it might seem like you just can't win. In the Old Testament, God's people fought some big armies they thought they would never overcome. But God is for the "little guy"—he's for you when it seems like you won't come out on top. And the minute you think you can't do something, he is there to help you. You won't magically get As on all of your tests, but he will help you work through whatever problem you're facing. Call out to him today, and he will help you overcome.

Dear God, I'm feeling overwhelmed today. There's so much going on in my life and I feel so helpless sometimes. Help me find someone who can understand what I'm going through. Help me make it through this battle as the winner.

Do You Hear What I Hear?

For, "Whoever would love life and see good days must keep their tongue from evil and their lips from deceitful speech."
1 PETER 3:10

When you turn on the TV you might hear a lot of words streaming out of it. Some of them are good words and some are words that would probably get you in trouble at school.

The TV isn't the only place you might hear those words—you could hear them on the bus, in a store, or at home. When something goes wrong, those words might even come out of your mouth.

It's difficult once you've started the habit of cussing to stop, so if you don't use foul language it's better not to start. If those words are already a part of your everyday life you can pray and ask God to help you break the habit. Maybe you have a Christian friend who could also help keep you accountable for what you say. God wants to help you control the words that come out of your mouth—when you keep your language clean you'll be happy knowing that he's pleased with you.

Are you struggling with your words? Write a prayer asking God to help you use words that honor him.

DAY 82

Part of the Team

So we rebuilt The waLL TiLL aLL of iT reached half iTs height, for The people worked with aLL Their heart.

NEHEMIAH 4:6

When you're on a field trip it's important to follow the buddy system so you don't lose anyone. When you wander out on your own, it's possible you could get lost or hurt. There's safety in numbers—safety when you stick together with the people who care about you.

In the Old Testament, when God's people were trying to protect themselves from their enemies, they worked together to build a wall so they would be safe. Because they worked as a team they were able to build the wall. You need teamwork in every aspect of your life—you need it in friendships, you need it in sports and school, and you need it in your family. Are you a team player or do you want things your way? What can you do to help things run smoothly for the teams in your life?

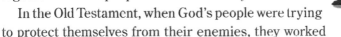

Write down one place it's hard for you to be a team player. Next time you start to argue, pause and think about keeping the peace so everyone can accomplish the common goal.

Diverse Is the New Cool

Now you are The body of ChrisT, and each one of you is a parT of iT.

1 Corinthians 12:27

What if you had a birthday party and every gift was identical? One by one you opened the presents, and one by one you realized that every guest brought the exact same thing.

Life is boring when everything's the same. You can't use twenty hoverboards, video games, or even graphic tees. In the same way, life would be boring if you and your friends were exactly the same. Instead, God made each of you different because he delights in diversity. The Bible says that you and your friends are like parts of a body—a skeleton working together to move. No body part is more important than the other, just different. One of your friends might make a great class president and another might be good at planning the campaign. One friend might be great at directing a play and another might make a great stagehand. What's your gift? Is it organizing things or running up front? Whatever you do well, it's needed. Up front or behind the scenes, you're an important part of the diversity God created.

Thank God for giving you the gift of being you today. Thank him that no matter how big or small your talent seems to be, it's important—and that's why he gave it to you!

Stones to Remember

Joshua set up the twelve stones that had been in the middle of
the Jordan at the spot where the priests who carried the ark of
the covenant had stood. And they are there to this day.
JOSHUA 4:9

Have you ever had a bad dream that woke you in the middle of the night? Maybe you were so scared your heart was pounding and your head was spinning. You might have prayed and asked God to help you feel better and help you get back to sleep.

Bad dreams are just one thing God can help you with. He can also help you when you're fighting with a friend, worried about a family member, or stressing about a test. When you get through that tough spot it's easy to forget that he's the one who helped you get to the other side.

In the Bible, God's people set up huge stones to remind them of the times God helped them through something. The rocks were a visual reminder of his help. You don't have to set up a huge rock in your backyard so you'll remember God's power in your life. Next time God gets you through a rough spot you could write about it inside your Bible flap or put sticky notes on your bathroom mirror. Then when times get tough you can go back and read about how God has helped you and always will.

Dear God, thank you for giving me courage in the past. Help me to always remember that it's you who gives me power to make it through the scary times. I love you.

DAY 85

Be Still and Know

He says, "Be still, and know that I am God; I will be exalted among the nations, I will be exalted in the earth."
PSALM 46:10

When you have a best friend you want to spend all your time with them. You probably beg your parents for sleepovers, movies, and after-school hangouts. You might go everywhere together—it's like the old saying that you're "attached at the hip." Everyone knows you are best friends because you even start acting like each other.

If you want to know God better you can treat him like a best friend. He's always with you and you can talk to him any time at all. Just like you do with your best friend, you'll want to make sure to plan intentional time with God too. What's your best time of day? If you wake up early you can plan a few minutes to read your Bible. Maybe you can take some time after homework to tell him what's on your mind. Or at night as you're falling asleep you can talk to God about your day. The more time you spend with him, the more others will notice that you're acting just like him. He's there, waiting, just asking for you to be still and remember that he's your God.

You're spending time with God just by reading this devotional book! Keep up the good work! Sit down every day and read, so you can hang out with your best friend.

King for a Day

Yours, Lord, is The greatness and The power and The glory and The majesty and The splendor, for everyThing in heaven and earth is yours. Yours, Lord, is The kingdom; you are exalTed as head over all.

I Chronicles 29:11

What would it be like to be king for a day? Kings in ancient times were called "sovereigns" because they were sovereign—in charge of—everything in their kingdoms. While presidents have limitations over what they do, most kings were able to run things however they wanted.

Did you know that God is sovereign over his kingdom too? Nothing happens in the world that he doesn't see or understand. Because of his goodness he allows people to reject him or accept him, and some people choose evil instead of good. Despite those choices, God still loves his people and wants the best for them. You might not get to be king for a day but you do get to know the king. He loves you and wants you to know that one day you'll live in a perfect kingdom with him—a kingdom where there will be no more sin or sadness. Until then you can trust your king because he is sovereign and over all—even the things you don't understand.

Thank you, Jesus, for being my king. Help me trust you when I don't understand what's going on in my life. One day I will understand, but until then—I choose to believe you're in control.

He's Everywhere

Who can hide in secret places so that I cannot see them?" declares
The Lord. "Do not I fill heaven and earth?" declares The Lord.
JEREMIAH 23:24

The Bible is filled with stories of people who tried to hide from God: Jonah, who hid on a boat; Adam and Eve, who hid in a garden; and Elijah, who hid in a cave, to name a few. It might seem strange to try to hide from God when he's everywhere, but sometimes we do the same thing without realizing it.

You might not try to hide from God by climbing under your bed or into your luggage (King Saul did that!), but you might try to avoid him by not going to church or not reading your Bible. Maybe you've made choices you know are wrong so you just try to pretend like he's not even around. The good news is that no matter how far you stray from God, he's always there loving you. The one who created galaxies we can't even see inhabits every square inch he made—and that includes you. He cares about you too much to let you go. Will you talk to him today?

Dear God, thank you for being omnipresent—everywhere. Thank you for being in my life. I don't want to make decisions without thinking of you. Please help me to follow you.

Where Two or Three

For where two or three gather in my name, there am I with them.
MATTHEW 18:20

What do you like to do when you hang out with friends? Maybe you play video games, run around outside, or jump on the trampoline. But what about when one of you is having a hard day? Maybe worrying about parents, homework, or even a sick pet.

If you have Christian friends God says you can pray with them when you're worried. He says when you have trouble you can ask him, and he'll be with you and your friends. When even two Christians are together Jesus says it's a great time to pray and ask him to help. You don't have to be at church to pray with a friend—you can pray anywhere. You don't have to make a big show of it either—you don't even have to bow your head and close your eyes (although that will help keep you from getting distracted). You can stop right where you are and ask your friend to talk to God with you, or you can ask to pray for your friend. Jesus is right there waiting to hear from you.

Do you have a friend who's struggling right now? Are you struggling right now? Next time you're with that friend, ask them to pray with you. Jesus hears the prayers of his kids.

He Gets the Credit

For from him and Through him and for him are aLL Things. To him be
The gLory forever! Amen.

ROMANS 11:36

When God created the first man it was pretty obvious he'd done an amazing thing: after all, he used dirt to make a person! When we see pregnant mamas walking around today it's easy to forget that the way God creates people now is every bit as amazing. He deserves a lot of recognition for what he does.

What brings you recognition? Are you good at reading, math, or debate? Can you tell a story that makes your friends sit with their mouths open? Are you the class clown who makes everyone laugh? Ask yourself: do you take credit when you do something really awesome? God is the one who made you and gave you every ability you have. When someone compliments you are you willing to acknowledge that *he's* the one who deserves the credit for giving you your abilities? Without him you wouldn't be able to sit, speak, or even think. In fact, you wouldn't even be alive! So next time someone tells you how amazing you are, remember to give credit to the one who gave you your abilities.

Dear God, thank you for creating me for your glory. Help me remember that you are the one who deserves all the credit. In Jesus' name, amen.

Don't Be a Hypocrite

These people honor me with their lips, but their hearts are far from me. They worship me in vain; their teachings are merely human rules.

MATTHEW 15:8–9

Have you ever known someone who attended church but didn't act like a Christian? Some people call it being a "Sunday Christian"—only acting like a Christian one day a week. Jesus called it being a hypocrite—saying one thing with your lips but doing another thing with your body.

The Bible says it's easy to use your words to honor God but your life might not match up. You could say you're a Christian but still use bad language. You could talk about Jesus but not help the poor. You could follow all the rules but still not have love for God in your heart. Your heavenly Father doesn't look just at what you do as a measurement for how much you love him. He looks at your heart and what motivates you. He wants you to spend time with him, not so you can check it off your list for the day, but because you love him. What's motivating you? Do you love God, or are you just using your words to say you do?

Dear God, I want to love you with more than just my words and actions—I want my heart to love you too. Help me spend time with you and grow in my love for who you are. Keep me from being a hypocrite.

Grace for Others

For it is by grace you have been saved, through faith—and this is not from yourselves, it is the gift of God—not by works, so that no one can boast.

EPHESIANS 2:8-9

Have you ever been wronged by a friend? Maybe they said something that hurt your feelings or broke one of your favorite things. Maybe they gossiped about you or didn't invite you to their party. Were you angry? Or did you forgive them?

God says we've broken his laws—every one of us. But even though we've all made bad choices, God decided to give us something we don't deserve: grace. When he sent his son to die for our sins, we received forgiveness. Because of God's grace, we can choose to give grace to others. When someone hurts us, we can choose not to stay angry. We might not feel they deserve forgiveness, but we don't deserve God's grace either. Who can you show grace to today?

Dear God, thank you for your grace. Thank you for forgiving me when I don't deserve it. Help me to forgive others, even my enemies. In Jesus' name, amen.

Making it Right

Do not steal. Do not lie. Do not deceive one another.
LEVITICUS 19:11

Have you ever looked at something someone else had and really, really wanted it? It could have been a softball glove, a T-shirt, or even something as simple as a piece of candy. Did you reach out and take it? Did you think about it all day?

Our bodies tell us when we've done something wrong—we feel nervous, agitated, and maybe even a little sick to our stomachs. That feeling is called guilt, and it comes because God says we shouldn't take things—or want to take things—that don't belong to us. When we do something like sneaking a pack of gum in the checkout line, we sin against God and we cheat someone else. The good news is we don't have to keep it as our little secret. We can make it right. We can return what we've stolen and apologize for what we've done. And next time, we can ask God to give us the strength to be happy with what we have.

Is there something you need to make right today? Can you go to that person and admit that you were wrong?

DAY 93

Who Goes First?

For the entire law is fulfilled in keeping this one command: "Love your neighbor as yourself."

GALATIANS 5:14

If you're standing in the cafeteria and the lunch line opens, do you rush to the front? What about in gym when the basketballs hit the floor—do you grab the first one or do you let someone else have a turn? At home, do you snatch the remote from your sister's hands or do you let her watch her favorite show?

Taking turns isn't easy. What do you do when it's so hard to share or to wait your turn? God says with his help you can love someone else just as much as you love yourself. If you ask him to give you patience, he'll show you how to wait for your turn. You'll be surprised at how happy it will make someone else when you let them go first. Jesus put us first—he can help you do the same for someone else.

Dear God, it's hard to wait for my turn. It's easier to jump in there and get what I need when I need it. Help me to pause and wait for someone else to have a turn. Help others to see Jesus in me when I practice taking turns. Amen.

Practice Makes Perfect

Whatever your hand finds to do, do it with all your might.
ECCLESIASTES 9:10A

Have you ever been in the middle of a long job and suddenly felt stuck? Maybe you were writing a paper, raking leaves, or going for a run. You started out enthusiastically but suddenly you lost your motivation and you weren't sure how to find it again.

Everyone gets tired sometimes. You might have a dream of doing something really big like winning a race or being first chair in your school band. Anything worth doing takes a lot of time and practice, and some people give up before they achieve their goals. The Bible says that if you find something you really want to do, you should do it with all your might—with everything inside you. This means you need to practice even when you don't feel like it. When you keep going when others have given up, you can achieve your goals. With God's help and your diligence, you can do anything God asks.

Write down that one thing you really want to do. Make a plan to set aside time to practice that skill. Follow your plan and don't give up—keep working with all your might.

Heart Soil

BuT The seed on good soil sTands for Those wiTh a noble and good hearT, who hear The word, reTain iT, and by persevering produce a crop.

LUKE 8:15

How's your soil today? What's that—you don't have a garden? God says you do. It's not made of real soil—it's made up of what you believe about him. He wants to plant truth in that garden, but truth only grows in a certain type of soil.

In the Bible, Jesus talks about different types of "soil" you can have in your heart, but only one of them is the type that will listen to God's Word, remember it, and obey it. That means when you go to church, you should not only listen to what's being said, but remember the message and follow it. (If you don't have anyone to take you to church, you can still learn about God's Word just by reading this devotional book.) When the soil in your heart is good, your life will grow good things—like a love for others and a love for God. Your friends will notice a positive difference in you, and God will be pleased with your heart that believes in truth and grows good things. What type of soil will you have today?

Dear God, I want your truth to grow in my heart. Help me to not only listen to your word, but to remember and obey it. Amen.

A Good Kind of Spirit

And I will ask the Father, and he will give you another advocate
to help you and be with you forever—the Spirit of Truth.
JOHN 14:16–17A

Where do you go when you have a problem? Maybe you look for your parents, a school guidance counselor, or a friend. If you have a cell phone, you probably have the people you trust on your favorites list.

There are times, though, when you need advice and you just can't find anyone to help. You could pick up your phone, but it might be 1 a.m. and way too late to be texting. Your parents might be cranky if you go wake them up.

But there's another option. Did you know that Jesus said he left someone with you who can help you any time? Since Jesus isn't with you physically, his spirit is inside you. That spirit can help you understand what you read in the Bible, so you know what to do when you have a problem. So next time it's dark and quiet and you don't know where to go, read your Bible. Talk to the Holy Spirit. He'll show you what to do. He'll never let you down.

Dear God, thank you for sending the Holy Spirit to live inside me. Thank you for comforting me and helping me find the answers I need. Help me remember to turn to your Holy Spirit first when I need help. Amen.

She Doesn't Have as Much

And do not forget to do good and to share with others, for with such sacrifices God is pleased.

HEBREWS 13:16

Do you know someone who doesn't have as much as you? Maybe she doesn't say anything about it, but there's not a lot of food in her lunchbox. Her clothes might be a little worn or her shoes might be too small. You want to help her, but how do you do it without making her feel bad about having less?

Don't just walk up to her and hand her a five-dollar bill (that could make her feel like you think she needs charity). Instead, start by being her friend. Kindness can mean even more than money. As you two get to know each other, you can find ways to help with the food in her lunchbox or those too small shoes. It may be by sharing your own lunch or saving up to help her buy some new sneakers. God says when you share with people who are in need, he'll reward you, and you'll feel happy to have a new friend.

Think of someone you know who doesn't have as much as you. What can you do to help that person feel taken care of? Write down your ideas and pick the best one to try tomorrow.

When it Doesn't Make Sense

By faith Noah, when warned about things not yet seen, in holy fear built an ark to save his family.
HEBREWS 11:7A

What if someone told you to build a giant boat and you live in the desert? What if someone said there'd be a huge flood but right now, the sun is shining? Would you believe it? Or would you laugh and keep right on doing what you are doing?

Almost every Christian has doubts about God's commands sometimes (probably even Noah, the man in the story about the boat). But rather than listening to those doubts, you can be like Noah. You can choose to believe with your heart even when there are doubts in your mind. If you have serious questions about the Bible, you can always ask your pastor or a Christian adult you know. They're happy to help you understand so that you can keep on learning and believing in God. What can you do today to be like Noah?

Dear God, help me to ask you for help when I don't understand or when I have doubts about you. Thank you for putting people in my life who can help me when I have hard questions. I choose to believe in you. Amen.

Careful of Your B.F.F.

As iron sharpens iron, so one person sharpens another.
PROVERBS 27:17

Who's your best friend? If you had to describe him, what words would you use? Would you say he's funny? Nice? Loyal? If your friend had to describe you, what do you think he would say?

The Bible says we should be careful who we hang out with, because when we spend all that time with one person, we start to pick up their habits. If your best friend is angry all the time you might start feeling angry too. If he likes to make fun of people, you might find yourself thinking of jokes in your head. If he likes to take stuff that doesn't belong to him, you might be tempted to do the same. On the other hand, if your friend loves people, you might find yourself thinking of ways to love others better. If he speaks kindly, you might think of nice words. And if he gives generously, you might think of ways to give to others. God says iron sharpens iron—in other words, the right friends can sharpen you into a better person. What kind of friends are you choosing? What type of person will you be?

Write down some words to describe your friends. Think about those words for a while—are those the things you want to become? If the answer is no, you might want to rethink the crowd you're spending time with.

DAY 100

So Much Stuff

For I have Learned To be conTenT whaTever The circumsTances.
PHILIPPIANS 4:11b

Have you noticed all the ads on social media lately? Every time you turn on the computer or your phone, someone's telling you about something you need. It's called marketing, and there are huge companies you can't see that have entire rooms of people trying to figure out what kids like you want. And with everything in the world, sometimes it's easy to want more and more and more.

The apostle Paul said he learned that whether he had a lot or a little, he could be content. His secret was that he realized stuff wasn't going to make him happy in the long run—only Jesus could do that. It's okay for you to own things—it's not okay for things to own you.

Are you always thinking of the next best device or game? Do you make long lists of what you'd like to get for your birthday or Christmas? Those might be signs that you're having a hard time with being happy with what you have. The good news is, you can ask God for help.

Dear God, help me to be happy with what I have. I don't want to always want more. You're the most important thing in my life—help me want to know you most of all.

DAY 101

Guests First

Offer hospitality to one another without grumbling.
I PETER 4:9

Hospitality's a funny word that doesn't have anything to do with going to the hospital. (Although if your parents say it's okay to visit the sick, that's a nice thing to do.) Being hospitable means making guests comfortable when you have them over to your house. So when you ask a friend to come hang out at your place, ask them what they'd like to do before making plans.

Things could go perfectly. Or . . . your friend might want to play basketball even if you hate basketball. They might want to watch a different movie than you had in mind. They might eat the last of your favorite snack or want to play some of your favorite games when you'd rather keep them to yourself.

Hospitality is choosing to be selfless when you really want to be selfish—and doing it without complaining. How can you be hospitable next time someone comes to your house?

Do you have plans to have a friend over sometime soon? What's one thing you can do to help them feel at home? Write that thing here and remember to practice it when they walk in the door.

Jelly on Your Homework?

Lazy hands make for poverty, but diligent hands bring wealth.
PROVERBS 13:4

Did you turn in your homework this morning with a little side of peanut butter and jelly on it? Does your locker smell like a can of sardines mixed with pickles? And when was the last time you actually washed your gym uniform?

Maybe you like everything neat and tidy, and if you do that's awesome. For some people, though, orderliness isn't something that comes easily—it takes practice. It's good when things are done in an orderly way. Think about how much time you could save if you didn't have to search for your permission slip or English paper. And what would your mom say if she walked past your bedroom door and discovered she could see the floor again? It might seem overwhelming to think about getting everything picked up, but if you start a little bit at a time you can do it. And you might find that you enjoy having less stress!

Set a timer for ten minutes every day (hint: don't use your homework time) to pick up your room. Every time you use something, put it back in the right place. Before you know it, your life will be in order and you'll feel good too.

Stand Firm in the Faith

Be on your guard; stand firm in the faith.

I Corinthians 16:13a

If you're playing defense in soccer or football, you're watching out for the other team. Your job is to keep the other team from scoring, so you can't take a nap or daydream.

God says you should watch out for temptation. If you're already looking for it, you won't be surprised when it shows up. You can be watching for temptation in the checkout line when you really want to take that pack of bubble gum. You can be watching for temptation when your friends gossip. And you can be watching for temptation when your mom tells you to do something and you want to be disrespectful back.

When you know how to resist temptation, you'll be ready for anything.

Dear God, thank you for helping me watch out for temptation. Thank you for giving me strength to do the right thing! I love you. In Jesus' name, amen.

Oh, So Tired

BuT Those who hope in The Lord will renew Their strength. They
will soar on wings Like eagLes; They will run and noT grow
weary, They will waLk and noT be faint.

ISAIAH 40:31

Have you ever felt exhausted? Maybe you stayed up all night at a sleepover or read a book with a flashlight under your covers. You could have gone swimming all day, or sat out in the hot sun by the lake. All of these things suck the energy right out of your body, and only rest will help you feel better.

Did you know your heart can be tired too? Not the heart beating inside of your chest, but the spiritual one God gave you. Your heart might be tired because you had a bad day, you've been working really hard to help a friend, or you're struggling with losing a loved one. It's okay. We all have times when we're tired. Next time you feel like you're empty inside and just don't have anything left to give, know that it's okay to give your heart a rest. Take a step back and spend time with God. He can renew your energy so you can feel like you again.

When was the last time you had a chance to rest? Reading this book is a great start, but don't forget to take some time out to think and rest too. Both your body *and* your spirit need those times of renewal so you can be at your best.

All Promised Out

Suppose one of you wants to build a tower. Won't you first sit down and estimate the cost to see if you have enough money to complete it?

LUKE 14:28

Do you collect stuff? Maybe it's video games, puzzles, or books. Maybe there's an entire collection of sports equipment in your garage. Do you save your money for some of those things, or do your parents buy them for you?

If you buy things for yourself, you know what it's like to sort through your piggy bank or bank account to see if there's enough for what you want. Can you afford it? How much longer will you need to save? Time is a lot like money—you only get so much of it. If you make too many promises like at school, sports, church, debate club, and on and on—you'll end up with no energy to keep your commitments. That's why it's important to sit down and make a list of what comes first for you and your family.

What's your favorite activity? What's your least favorite? If you count the cost before you make plans, you'll find yourself a lot less stressed and with a lot more energy to do the things you love.

Are you using your time well or do you feel stressed out by having too much on your schedule? If you're feeling stressed, maybe you could read this devotional with your parents and talk about it.

Praying God's Will

"Father, if you are willing, take this cup from me; yet not my will, but yours be done."

LUKE 22:42

Have you ever asked God to do something and the opposite happened? Maybe you asked him to heal a friend, but that friend is still sick. Maybe you prayed for a better grade and despite all your studying, it just didn't happen. All of these things are painful and sometimes feel like they don't make sense.

Jesus prayed for something, too, and the opposite happened. The night before he died on the cross, he asked God to "take this cup from me"—to take away his pain and suffering. Then he ended his prayer with, "yet not my will, but yours be done". It was hard for Jesus to pray this prayer, but he knew God had a bigger purpose. If Jesus didn't die on the cross, we couldn't be saved from our sin. Jesus set the example for us when he taught us to pray for God's will instead of ours. When you ask God to do his will, you can know he has a bigger plan than you can imagine.

Dear God, I trust your plan when I pray for your will. Sometimes my will and yours will be the same—other times they won't. I'm glad you know what you're doing even when I don't see or understand your plan.

No Measuring, Please

So when you, a mere human being, pass judgment on them and yet do the same things, do you think you will escape God's judgment?
ROMANS 2:3

Some people like macaroni and cheese and other people like pizza. Some like broccoli and some like carrots. Some people eat brownies and others prefer hot fudge sundaes.

God says we all have differences, right down to how we understand the Bible. Your family might believe in taking communion at church every week, and your friend might believe in taking it once a month. Or you might wear jeans to church, and your friend might dress like they're going to a funeral. None of these things measures how much you love God—in fact, he says you shouldn't judge each other based on how you worship him. Judging goes all the way back to Bible days when Christians argued with each other about what they were allowed to eat. But God says it's okay to have differences. We don't have to judge. We don't have to measure how much we love him. We can just know that we're all a little different and that's okay. We can also celebrate the things we do have in common. We're God's family, and we're in this together!

God, I don't want to be judgmental of my friends. I want to love and accept them for where they are in their relationship with you. Help me to remember to ignore the things that don't matter and focus on the things that do. Amen.

DAY 108

Late Again?

Be devoted to one another in love. Honor one another above
yourselves.

ROMANS 12:10

Does your mom call you six times before you roll out of bed? Do you stumble to the breakfast table and mumble a few words when she says the bus is on its way? Are you still brushing your teeth when the horn honks outside?

When you're late for school you're not only signing in tardy, but you're failing to show respect to your teacher. When you don't show up on time for your brother's soccer game, you're failing to show him love. And when you miss youth group at church, you're failing to show your friends honor. Being on time takes self-discipline. It means getting out of bed the first time mom calls, showing up when you say you will, and leaving for practice on time even when you're doing something more interesting.

When you show respect for others' time, you're honoring God and loving others—and that's exactly what you hope others will do for you.

What's one thing you can change today so you can honor someone's time? Write it down and put it in a place where you'll see it every day. The more you practice being on time, the better you'll be at it.

Your Day Interrupted

And the Lord's servant must not be quarrelsome but must be kind to everyone.

2 TIMOTHY 2:24A

Can you make a fist? Stretch your fingers out again? Push your hand toward the sky? Can your thumb touch your wrist? How flexible is your body?

Did you know that your attitude can be flexible too? That's right—you can bend it in the direction you want it to go. You might have woken up this morning expecting to see cereal on the table, but there were eggs instead. Maybe you thought you'd play volleyball after school, but your friends wanted to play hockey. Or maybe you were hoping for an easy morning in English class, but your teacher whipped out a pop-quiz.

Being flexible—willing to change your plans when it's important—is a great quality to have. It doesn't mean you have to be a pushover or always give in (especially not when it comes to issues that bother your conscience). It just means realizing when something's a big deal and when it's not. Are you willing to have your plans interrupted? Or do you always have to have things your way?

Dear God, I don't want to always have to have things my way. I want to think of others and what they might need too. Help me to be flexible with my plans. In Jesus' name, amen.

The Father of Lies

For There is no Truth in him. When he Lies, he speaks his native
Language, for he is a Liar and The father of Lies.

JOHN 8:44B

Have you ever known a person you couldn't trust? You may have believed that person the first few times she told you something, but after a while you figured out she rarely spoke the truth. Pretty soon you learned not to believe anything.

From the beginning of time, Satan has been a liar. You can always tell when he tries to lie to you, because the thoughts in your head will be the opposite of what God says in his Word. Satan might try to tell you that no one cares about you, but the Bible says God does. He might try to tell you you're not attractive, but the Bible says you're created in God's image (you can't get more attractive than that!). He might try to tell you you're worthless, but the Bible says you're so full of worth that Jesus died on the cross for you. Whenever a thought comes that makes you feel bad about yourself, compare it to what God says—that's the ultimate truth test.

Write down some negative thoughts you've had about yourself in the past. Next to those thoughts, write down what God says. Whenever you're feeling down, go back and look at that sheet of paper. The one who created you is the one who tells you the truth.

The Gift of Earth

Then God said, "Let us make mankind in our image, in our likeness, so that they may rule over the fish in the sea and the birds in the sky, over the livestock and all the wild animals,[a] and over all the creatures that move along the ground."

GENESIS 1:26

What if you gave your best friend a really expensive basketball for his birthday? Maybe he was super excited about it and thanked you for it. But the next time you went to his house, the ball was deflated and dirty. He'd left it outside and forgotten about it.

God's given us a wonderful gift that we sometimes forget to take care of too. It's better than a basketball—it's the world! We only get one earth, and we're in charge of taking care of it. There are lots of ways we can do this—from volunteering at a pet shelter to picking up trash by the side of the road. Even small things like recycling our plastic goods can make a huge difference if enough of us do it. Keeping God's earth clean and cared for is a sign of respect for him, and it's healthier for all of us too. What can you do to help take care of God's world?

Write down some ideas for keeping the earth healthy. Then pick one and start there. Even small steps make big differences.

One Bite at a Time

ALL hard work brings a profit, but mere talk leads only to poverty.
PROVERBS 14:23

Your mom tells you to clean your room but you feel overwhelmed. Maybe you stall by saying you have soccer practice or homework. Eventually you run out of excuses. It's so bad in there you're pretty sure you saw a mammoth spider under your bed, but you were too afraid to investigate. Stacks of homework litter your floor mingled with dirty socks and soccer cleats (and let's not even get started on the smell).

Maybe this doesn't sound like you at all—maybe your room is sparkling clean, but there are other things overwhelming you. You might need to write a long paper or run a relay at a track meet. Whatever's hanging over you, there's only one way to approach it: one step at a time. How do you run a race? By putting one foot in front of the other. Just start working on your goals and you'll make progress. After you reach your first small goal, set another. Be consistent and work a little on your project every day. Before you know it, with God's strength, your task will be finished and you'll feel accomplished.

Write down a goal that's overwhelming you. Now break it down into smaller steps. Follow those steps until you're finished!

Putting on Your Glasses

Then you will know the truth, and the truth will set you free.
JOHN 8:32

Do you know someone who wears glasses or contacts? Maybe it's you. What happens when you go without them? Perhaps things are just a little blurry, or maybe you can't see anything at all. When you can't see where you're going, that means you've lost your perspective.

Sometimes we lose our perspective in other ways too. When something bad happens, it's easy to let it ruin your day. You might get three compliments and one put-down, and your brain will only remember that negative comment.

The good news is, you can find your perspective again by picking up your Bible and reading what God has to say about who you are. When you see that you're loved, special, and uniquely gifted—it's like putting your glasses on. So no matter what happens in your day, or how people treat you, you can always come back to the truth—God will help you see clearly.

God, help me put on my glasses today by reading your Word. Help me to believe what the Bible says instead of what other people say. Amen.

Good Medicine

A cheerful heart is good medicine, but a crushed spirit dries
up the bones.

PROVERBS 17:22

When you look at the future, what do you see? Do you have hopes?
Dreams? What do you want to be?

The Bible says that a cheerful heart—an optimistic outlook—is like
good medicine. When you look into the future with excitement, you're
bringing happiness to yourself. When you look to the future with dread,
your spirit—what you think and feel on the inside—dries up and loses
hope. Maybe you've had some tough things happen recently. Maybe life hit
you hard and you're still recovering. It's okay to feel sad if you're dealing
with difficult circumstances. But at some point you need to start dreaming
again. If you can be optimistic about things getting better, they will. You
have good things ahead of you on this adventure, and working toward a
cheerful attitude will push you in the right direction. Trust God and know
that he wants to give you the gift of an optimistic, cheerful heart.

Make a dream list of what you'd like to see in your future. What goals
can you work toward? Just making plans with optimism can give you a
cheerful heart.

Strong & Powerful

For The word of God is alive and active. Sharper Than any double-edged sword, iT penetrates even To dividing souL and spiriT, joints and marrow; iT judges The ThoughTs and aTTiTudes of The hearT.
HEBREWS 4:12

It's day 115 of reading this devotional—have you noticed how thoughts from it pop into your head sometimes? Maybe someone's being mean to you and you remember the part about loving your enemies. Maybe you're feeling lonely and you remember a verse about God always being with you. Maybe you're complaining and remember the page about being grateful instead.

God's word is powerful. It changes the way you think and act. It's so strong that it's like a sword, dividing your thoughts and helping you sort out truth from lies. Just by picking up this devotional and your Bible every day, you're choosing a huge adventure with God. Part of that adventure might even be reading the chapters that go with the verses at the beginning of these devotionals. God wants to walk with you every step of the way of this adventure, and he does that when you read his Word. Keep reading, keep remembering, and keep living out this journey with God.

What's one way God's changed your attitude through reading his Word? Write it down in your Bible. Every time you notice him helping you make good choices, record it there and thank him for his work in your life.

Take a Deep Breath

So do not fear, for I am with you; do not be dismayed, for I am your God. I will strengthen you and help you; I will uphold you with my righteous right hand.

ISAIAH 41:10

What makes you feel frustrated? Maybe it's when your parents don't understand what you're trying to say, when your brother or sister tries their best to get on your nerves, or when you don't understand your homework.

Frustration can make you feel like yelling or slamming your bedroom door. It can make you feel like running away from your problem. It can even make you feel like beating your pillow with your fists. All these feelings are natural emotions that even adults get sometimes. But what do you do when those emotions get the best of you? It's okay to step away from your problem for a while until you feel better. Take a deep breath and tell God how you feel. Go for a walk, play a game, or read a book. When you're feeling better come back to your parents, or your sibling, or your homework. God wants to help you with your everyday emotions, including frustration. He cares about everything in your life.

Dear God, help me to remember that you want to help me with my frustration. Instead of yelling or running away, help me to bring my problems to you. I love you. Amen.

Lazing Around

Laziness brings on deep sleep, and the shiftless go hungry.
PROVERBS 19:15

Do you ever have problems that seems too tough to solve? You're working through your piano piece, but there's one section that you just can't figure out. Your math problem is long and complicated. You can't find your lunchbox and you've looked everywhere.

Your first thought might be to give up or to ask your mom for help. But what if you tried for just a little while longer? What if you took that piano piece or math problem and worked on it one step at a time? What if you looked just a little while longer for your lunchbox? When you work hard to tackle a problem on your own, you're being independent—an important part of growing up. It's okay to ask for help if you really need it, but you should make sure you're not just taking a shortcut. When you do work for yourself even when it's tough, you'll feel good when you figure it out on your own. What task can you tackle today on your own?

Next time you're having trouble solving a problem, give yourself some time to think it through. Work through ideas and try different tactics. Don't be lazy—whenever possible, learn how to figure it out for yourself!

DAY 118

Are You Listening?

No one should seek their own good, but the good of others.
I CORINTHIANS 10:24

What if you had a friend who always talked about himself? What if when you told him something awesome happened in your life, he had to top it with something better that happened to him? What if you got a new skateboard but he had to tell you how much better his is?

People who always have to turn a conversation toward themselves are acting self-focused. They might not realize it, but they're making it all about them. We all have the capability to be self-focused. The more we grow, though, the more we should begin to stop and think about giving our friends the spotlight sometimes. Are you accidentally talking about yourself a lot? Having a conversation should be like hitting a tennis ball—one person talks and then the other person talks. Learn to ask questions about your friends and you'll enjoy getting to know them better. They might even do the same for you! Are you seeking good for your friends, or is it all about you?

Practice taking turns in conversation at home. Ask your mom or dad how their day was, then let them ask you a question back.

The Perfect Specimen

My flesh and my heart may fail, but God is the strength of my heart and my portion forever.

PSALM 73:26

You're standing in line at the store and it's your turn to pay. You reach for the money in your back pocket and realize—some of it's gone. You're a few dollars short, and you're not sure what to do.

Maybe you've never lost money at the store, but you've come up short on other things. You studied hard but failed your test. You scored a soccer goal—for the other team. You bombed your violin recital. Everyone fails sometimes, and it's okay not to be perfect. No one in the whole world is perfect—why should you be? God says when things don't work out the way you plan, he makes up the difference. That doesn't mean you shouldn't give it your best effort. It just means that when you try your best and come up short, he'll give you grace. So next time you feel like you failed, trust that he loves you just the way you are.

Dear God, thank you for loving me even when I fail. Help me to remember that you're proud of me when I do my best. I love you. Amen.

What's Your Motive?

Everyone lies to their neighbor; they flatter with their lips but harbor deception in their hearts.

PSALM 12:2

Have you ever had someone compliment you but it didn't feel quite right? Some people will try to flatter you so you'll do something nice back for them. When someone does that it's called being insincere.

You should always say what you mean without trying to get something out of it. Don't do something nice for your mom because you're hoping she'll let you go to the sleepover tomorrow. Don't tell your teacher her hair looks nice so she'll like you a little better. And don't tell your friend she did a great job at the basketball game so she'll ask you to her birthday party. There's nothing wrong with giving a compliment—God loves it when we're kind to others. He's all about us using our words. But he also wants us to always stop and think about our motives. How can you be sincere today?

Jesus, help me to be sincere today. Help me to use my words to build others up in a way that's honest and true. In Jesus' name, amen.

DAY 121

Surprised by Jesus

Because They all saw him and were Terrified. Immediately he spoke To Them and said, "Take courage! IT is I. Don't be afraid."
MARK 6:50

Have you ever walked around the corner to find someone there you didn't expect? You were minding your own business when all of a sudden—yikes! You felt like jumping out of your skin. You might've even been so surprised you yelled.

The same thing happened to Jesus' disciples one dark night when they were fishing on the lake. The wind was whipping, the boat was tossing, and the lightning was flashing. As if they weren't terrified enough by the storm, suddenly there was a ghost on the water! Only it wasn't a ghost—it was Jesus. In the middle of their fear, they were surprised to find him there.

You never need to be surprised to find Jesus helping you in the middle of your fear. Whatever's worrying you today—sickness, loss of friendships, even frightening TV shows you maybe shouldn't have watched—Jesus is there with you. He says don't be afraid—it's just him. Don't be startled—he's your friend. And don't be worried—he has this all under control.

Thank you, Jesus, for being with me when things get scary. I don't have to be afraid because you're here. I give you my fear. Amen.

DAY 122

Getting Heated

Now about your love for one another we do not need to write to you, for you yourselves have been taught by God to love each other.

I THESSALONIANS 4:9

What gets you heated? Do you argue with your parents about homework? Do you argue with your siblings when they take your stuff? Do you argue with your friends about the other people they're hanging out with? There are a million things to argue about, and some of us are more argumentative than others.

Conflict is a normal part of life, but it's important to fight fair. That means not raising your voice or calling people names. It means waiting your turn then sharing your point of view. And sometimes (when it's not an adult you're arguing with) it means realizing you might never agree, and that's okay. There are billions of people in the world, and not every person is going to have the same point-of-view. So next time you disagree with someone you care about, remember to treat them fairly and, most importantly, kindly. The world could use a whole lot more of that.

Dear God, help me to treat others with kindness even when I don't agree with them. Give me love for people who have other points of view. Amen.

All Stressed Out

Cast all your anxiety on him because he cares for you.
1 Peter 5:7

Have you ever had one of those days when everything happened at once? Your sports game, your pop-quiz, your church service, your recital, and the mountain of homework your math teacher decided was perfect for that night? There's so much to do, and before you know it you're snapping at your mom and yelling at your sister, and you know it's because—hey—wait—did you remember to eat lunch today? One more thing to add to your list.

Busy days are hard, and it's even harder to stay calm under pressure. When you find yourself being short or angry with others, you can turn to God instead. Take a deep breath and tell him how you're feeling. He says you can cast your anxiety on him, because he cares for you. Give your stress to Jesus. When you're finished praying, you can come back to your sports, pop-quiz, church service, recital, and homework feeling a little lighter.

God, I give my stress to you. Thank you for caring about me. When I feel like lashing out at others, help me to come to you as my safe place. In Jesus' name, amen.

Hiding God's Word

I have not departed from the commands of his lips; I have
treasured the words of his mouth more than my daily bread.
JOB 23:12

What do you do when you have a treasured possession? Do you keep it
close to you? Protect it from others? Think about it a lot?

God says we should treasure his words. That doesn't mean you have to
carry your Bible everywhere (but you can if you want to)—you can have
God's words in your heart too. In the Bible, King David said he hid God's
words there—in his heart—so he would remember not to sin against God.

How do you hide God's word in your heart? By memorizing it. You
don't have to start memorizing in Genesis and end in Revelation—that
would be a lot of work! Pick some verses that you like, especially ones that
tell you what to do when you need help (you can even pick some out of
this devotional book). Make a list of two or three verses, and start there.
When you're in trouble and not sure what to do, those verses will come
back to your mind and help you figure it out. Where will you start?

Write a verse on a sticky note and put it on your mirror or somewhere
you'll see it every day. You can also put it in the front of a school book
where you can look at it any time. Memorize one sentence and then the
next. Before you know it, you'll know the whole verse!

DAY 125

Separate For a Purpose

King David dedicated These articles To The Lord, as he had done
with The silver and gold from all The nations he had subdued.
2 SAMUEL 8:11

When you go shopping for new school supplies, your mom probably tells you to keep them separate from the other things in your room. The pencils, pens, and paper are dedicated for homework—not for drawing, other artwork, or rubber band slingshots.

The word dedicated means intended for one purpose. When King David dedicated some of his possessions to God, it meant those things no longer belonged to him. You can dedicate lots of things to God—money, time, and possessions, just to name a few. But the most important thing you can dedicate to God is you—every plan and action. It's a wonderful feeling to be dedicated to someone you can trust, someone who wants to guide you to make wise choices. When you accepted Jesus as your savior, you probably told him that you wanted to be saved from your sin. But have you told him that you want to spend your life on an adventure dedicated to him? Would you like to do that today?

Dear God, thank you for saving me from my sin. I dedicate my life to you. I want to be set apart for your plans. I trust you. Amen.

Putting on a Good Attitude

Therefore, as God's chosen people, holy and dearly loved, clothe yourselves with compassion, kindness, humility, gentleness and patience.

COLOSSIANS 3:12

When you get up in the morning, what kind of clothes do you put on? Maybe you have a school uniform, or maybe you pull on your favorite pair of jeans and a T-shirt. Do you lay your clothes out the night before, or do you pick them up from a heap on the floor?

God says you can plan what you want to wear every day—not just your physical clothes, but with a good attitude. He wants you to be compassionate, kind, humble, gentle, and patient. That's a tall order, but he can help you do it when you ask. To be compassionate, you can listen to a friend who's hurting. To be kind, you can do something nice for someone. To be humble, you can choose not to brag. To be gentle, you can walk away from an argument. And to be patient, you can wait in line without complaining. What are some other ways you can dress yourself with a good attitude today?

Dear God, before I even roll out of bed in the mornings, help me get dressed with the most important thing—a good attitude. Help me to be compassionate, kind, humble, gentle, and patient. In Jesus' name, amen.

133

He Deserves It

And again, "Praise the Lord, all you Gentiles; let all the peoples extol him."

ROMANS 15:11

What do you think of when you hear the words, "Praise the Lord?" Do you think of raising your hands in worship at church? Do you think of shouting? Do you think of singing quietly? What does it mean, exactly, to praise him?

Praising God means to give him credit for how amazing he is. In the Bible, God's people lifted up huge banners of praise for everyone to see. You don't have to lift up a banner or fall on your knees when you're thanking God; you can do whatever feels natural to you. You don't have to be in church, and you don't have to be having a good day. You can praise him in good weather and in bad. You can praise him when you make the team, and when you don't. You can praise him when you're happy, and when you're sad. The most important thing is to praise him no matter what.

How are you feeling today? Even if you're down-and-out, you can praise God that he is who he is, and he always keeps his promises. Write down a praise, sing one, or even silently pray one. He's worthy of your praise!

Cheap Imitations

Dear friend, do not imitate what is evil but what is good. Anyone who does what is good is from God. Anyone who does what is evil has not seen God.

3 John 1:11

What if you knew a cat that barked like a dog? Or a chicken who mooed like a cow? Those things would probably never happen, but there is one animal—a parrot—that can imitate almost any other animal.

You don't have to be like a parrot—you don't have to imitate anyone else. In fact, God says to be different—to abstain from evil and to cling to what is good. When your friends are using bad language, arguing with their parents, or making fun of their teachers you don't have to join in. When they're picking on the small kids, looking at bad things on their phones, or listening to music with a parental advisory warning, you don't have to go along. You're created to be like God, not an imitation of someone else. God made you in his image. Who have you been imitating? How can you live like God instead?

Dear God, help me to imitate you. I want to do what's good. Thank you for creating me in your image. Amen.

Into the Clouds

After he said this, he was taken up before their very eyes, and a cloud hid him from their sight.

ACTS 1:9

Can you imagine—you're standing there talking to someone and suddenly they start levitating? They don't even have a hover board! They say their last words and slowly disappear into a cloud from the tip of their nose to the bottoms of their feet.

When Jesus ascended to heaven, that might be how it looked. After his death and resurrection, he told his friends he was going home to prepare a place for them. But guess what? He isn't staying there! One day, Jesus promises he'll come back to get everyone who believes in him—those who are alive and those who have already passed away. We don't know when he'll come back, but he always keeps his promises. What will you do in the meantime? The last thing he told his friends was that they should go into the world and tell everyone about him. You don't have to go that far, but you can pick one friend to tell about Jesus today. One day he's coming again!

Dear Jesus, thank you for going to heaven to prepare a place for me. Help me to tell my friends about you so they'll be ready, too, when you come again. In Jesus' name, amen.

No Gloating, Please

You should not gloat over your brother in the day of his misfortune, nor rejoice over the people of Judah in the day of their destruction, nor boast so much in the day of their trouble.
OBADIAH 1:12

Y ou're playing a video game and the goal is to take down the enemy. You might spend hours, even days, defeating level after level until finally you come out on top. The crowd goes wild (if you're the crowd, that is).

What about when it comes to enemies in real life? That girl who gossips about you? That guy who sends mean texts? That other guy who spreads lies about you on social media? You've tried your best, but there's no way to make peace with these enemies. Is it so wrong to laugh if one of them falls on his face in the lunchroom? Or is it mean to snicker if one of them has a bad breakup in the hallway? Did that person get what was coming to them? It's tempting to be happy when something bad happens to someone we don't like, but God says that rejoicing in their pain makes us no different than them. So instead of gloating when something bad happens to your enemy, try praying for them instead. You might find it changes your heart and makes you feel like the real winner.

Dear God, help me to love my enemies. Help me not to gloat when something bad happens to them, but to pray for them instead. Amen.

Faithful Friends

Many claim To have unfailing Love, buT a faithful person who can find?

PROVERBS 20:6

Have you ever had a friend who turned his back on you? Maybe he was nice to you for a long time—you did everything together. Now he acts like you don't exist. Or even worse, maybe he talks badly about you to your other friends.

Loyal friends are hard to find, but David found one in Jonathan. Even when Jonathan's dad, King Saul, became jealous of David and tried to kill him, Jonathan hid David and protected him. You might feel discouraged when no one wants to protect you—to be your loyal friend. Just because you've had one or even two rough friendships doesn't mean there aren't good ones too. When you're looking for a friend, search for someone who does and says kind things about everyone. That will be one of the first clues that you've found someone who will do and say nice things for you. Then try being the friend you want to have. A good friend may be hard to find, but the search is worth it in the end.

Dear God, please help me find a friend who's loyal and kind. Help me to be that kind of friend too. When I'm feeling friendless, you're with me.

Brown Sparrows

Are not two sparrows sold for a penny? Yet not one of
them will fall to the ground outside your Father's care.
MATTHEW 10:29

Sparrows like to hang out in parking lots, on rooftops, inside tree branches—pretty much everywhere. They're so common that many people don't notice them. Their feathers aren't bright red like the cardinal's or vibrant blue like the blue jay's—but God says even though the sparrows blend in, he notices them. As part of his creation, he cares for them.

If God notices the sparrows, you can be sure he notices you. When the whole world gets busy, God is watching you. He knows when you're feeling up, and when you're feeling down. He knows when you're doing right, and when you're doing wrong. He knows when you're winning and when you're losing. No matter what, God notices you, he loves you, and he cares for you. Just remember that next time you see a sparrow.

Dear God, thank you for noticing the sparrows. Thank you for doing more than notice them—you care for them, and you care for me. Help me to remember your loving care today. Amen.

DAY 133

Why So Flashy?

EveryThing They do is done for people To see.
MATTHEW 23:5A

In Jesus' day, church was a big show. Pharisees (religious leaders) stood up in the synagogue in flashy clothes and prayed long, fancy prayers. When they helped the poor they made sure everyone could see. Jesus said they did everything to get credit from people.

Don't fall into the same trap as the Pharisees—don't do good works so you'll be seen and praised by other people. If you're volunteering at a nursing home, you don't need to take selfies for social media. If you're going on a mission trip, you can probably leave your newest clothes at home. And if you're helping in the kids' program at church, you don't need to be the first one to volunteer to be up front. Does that mean you can never take pictures, dress confidently, or talk about volunteering? No. But what matters is what's in your heart. Is it all about you, or are you doing good things for people because you love them and God? What's your motive?

Dear God, help me do things out of love for others and for you. Thank you for loving me so that I can love others from my heart. Amen.

A Person After God's Own Heart

My sacrifice, O God, is a broken spirit; a broken and contrite heart you, God, will not despise.

PSALM 51:17

In the Bible, David sinned against God in two ways—by taking another man's wife and then by having that man killed. But somehow when God spoke about David he called him, "a man after my own heart." How could God say that about David when he'd done these terrible things?

David was completely broken by what he'd done. His heart was in pieces; he was shocked by his own sin. God still had to punish David's acts, but he was able to call him a man after his own heart because of David's repentance. When we repent from our sin we shouldn't just say, "I'm sorry" and be done. We should be shocked by what we've done; our hearts should be broken that we've broken God's heart. When we share his sadness it will motivate us to change our ways next time temptation comes. If you feel like you've sinned against God in unforgivable ways, know that your mistakes don't keep you from being a person after God's heart. He loves you and sees your desire to do what's right.

Dear God, help me to be truly sorrowful about my sin. Help me to be honest when I've disobeyed you. Thank you for your forgiveness, and your power to do what's right.

Those Who Are with You

"Don't be afraid," the prophet answered. "Those who are with us are more than those who are with them."

2 KINGS 6:16

Have you ever played the game capture the flag in the dark? Your goal is to sneak quietly across the other team's line and grab the flag when they're not looking. The tough part about playing in the dark is communicating with your teammates—you can't see them very well, even though you know they're still working with you.

Two prophets in the Bible were in a real war, and it looked like they were about to be captured. They could see each other, but they couldn't see the rest of God's team. Then God opened their eyes to see the millions of angels surrounding and protecting them. One prophet said to the other, "Those who are with us are more than those who are with them."

Whatever you're facing today, there are more with you than against. As God's child, you have an entire army of angels surrounding and defending you. When you feel outnumbered or bullied, remember that God is by your side—his angels are with you and they will keep you safe.

Dear God, thank you for keeping me safe. Thank you for surrounding me with your angels, even when I can't see them. Amen.

DAY 136

The Recipe

And we know that in all things God works for the good of those who love him, who have been called according to his purpose.
ROMANS 8:28

Have you ever begged your mom to make cookies? Together you gathered the flour, salt, sugar, baking soda, and other ingredients. You mixed them up into one goopy, gross-looking mess. None of those ingredients seemed very yummy on their own. You knew in the end, though, that something good was coming.

Something good was coming for God's people in the Bible too. When Paul wrote to them, he told them that even though they were suffering, God was working behind the scenes for their good. God's still the master chef and he still has something good coming out of your mess. Some ingredients in the recipe of your life might not make sense to you. He might allow some loss, some sadness, or some anger. He might allow you to miss the goal—to fail the test—to lose the friendship. But behind the scenes he has a plan, and even though you've tasted how bitter life can be, he has something sweet in store. You can trust that he's working it all together for your good.

Dear God, even when parts of my life don't make sense, I know you're working it together for good. I trust you. In Jesus' name, amen.

Miserable Comforters

"I have heard many things like these; you are miserable comforters, all of you!"

JOB 16:2

Have you ever told a friend your problems, but they didn't seem to understand? Maybe they only listened for a minute then offered a solution. Job, in the Bible, had friends like that. When his family died, his heart was broken. His friends came to see him and they cried with him and comforted him. But after they dried their eyes, they were quick to tell Job what he'd done to deserve all the pain he was going through. They judged him.

When you're comforting a friend, remember that you can't fully understand why God allows problems in some people's lives. It might seem clear to you what your friend's doing wrong, but God is the only one who really sees what's going on behind the scenes. If Job's friends had listened and loved instead of judging, they wouldn't have added more heartache on top of his loss. Don't be like Job's friends—don't be a miserable comforter. Instead strive to listen, care, and understand.

Dear God, help me to be a good comforter. Help me to show your love to my friends who are hurting. Take away my judgmental heart and give me one that only loves. Amen.

Your Name in Lights

Then they said, "Come, let us build ourselves a city, with a tower that reaches to the heavens, so that we may make a name for ourselves; otherwise we will be scattered over the face of the whole earth."

GENESIS 11:4

Do you want to be famous? Are you hoping to be a movie star, a pro athlete, or a musician? How cool would it be to stand in front of a huge crowd and be recognized for something you'd worked so hard to do?

There's nothing wrong with wanting to be famous if you're doing it because you want to give God glory. But if you're doing it because you want to build a name for yourself, you'll find that you can't compete with God. At the Tower of Babel, God's people built a monument to make a name for themselves. It didn't turn out well—God scattered them around the world and confused their language. He doesn't share the spotlight—he created you with your gifts and your abilities not to make you famous but to make him famous. How can you give him glory today?

Dear God, help me make you famous. Help me remember that you are the one who made the world and everything in it. You deserve the credit, and I give it to you. Amen.

Holding Up Your Hands

When Moses' hands grew tired, they took a stone and put it under him and he sat on it. Aaron and Hur held his hands up—one on one side, one on the other—so that his hands remained steady till sunset.

EXODUS 17:12

Have you ever had a hard day and someone offered to pray for you? Maybe it was a friend at school or your youth pastor at church. When they finished praying, you felt better because someone cared enough to listen.

When Moses was watching God's people fight a battle, he needed help too. He raised his hands in prayer, but eventually his arms were too tired to stay up. Every time his arms fell, the other army began to win. When he lifted them again, God's people were taking the victory. Moses' friends noticed how exhausted he was and sat on both sides of him to help hold up his arms. You, like Moses, need friends who will help you and pray for you when you're not feeling strong. That's why it's important to go to church if you can and make friends who will encourage you when things get tough. Have you been to church lately? Why not give it a try this weekend?

Dear God, I pray that you'll give me supportive friends like Moses had. I pray that we'll help each other when life gets hard. In Jesus' name, amen.

Only Watching the Ride

He set my feet on a rock and gave me a firm place to stand.
PSALM 40:2b

Have you ever watched a roller coaster? Up, then down, then up again—you know the riders' heads are spinning, but your feet are planted firmly on the ground. You're only watching the ride.

Sometimes your emotions are going to take you on a roller coaster. It might be because of changes in your body, or because of changes in your life. It could be a combination of both—but the ride might not feel like much fun at the time. How do you control your anger when you want to explode? What about when sadness comes out of nowhere? Who do you talk with when you feel like no one's listening?

You don't have to stay on the roller coaster of bad emotions. You can call on God to save you from it. David said when he was down that God "set my feet on a rock and gave me a firm place to stand." That rock was God. Next time you're feeling discouraged, ask him to help you get off the roller coaster and give you a firm place to stand.

Dear God, help me to stand firm on you, no matter what my emotions tell me. You're my rock—the one who never changes, even when I'm angry, sad, or scared. Thank you for never changing. Amen.

For Such a Time As This

And who knows but that you have come to your royal position for such a time as this?

ESTHER 4:14b

D id you know God placed you in this world at exactly the right time? You have a purpose that only you can fulfill. Your destiny was created by God himself, and only God can give you the courage you will need to make it happen.

Queen Esther knew what it was like to be courageous. She wasn't sure if she could save her people from being attacked, but she knew she had to  try—she had to ask her husband, the king, if he would help her defend the Jewish people. There was one problem, though. The king had a history of being angry for no reason, and he might order Esther to be killed if she came into his presence without being asked. But Esther braved it. She asked for his help, and she saved an entire nation as a result.

You might not save an entire nation, but God has big plans for you too. He's brought you to your school, your church, and your neighborhood for a purpose—to share his truth and love with others. It requires bravery, but with God's strength you can be like Esther. You are here "for such a time as this."

No Longer the Same

When Jesus reached The spot, he Looked up and said to him, "Zacchaeus, come down immediately. I must stay at your house Today."

LUKE 19:5

Imagine a grown man climbing a tree! When Jesus came around, shorter people couldn't see him because the crowd was too big. Zacchaeus, a tax collector who also stole peoples' money, decided that peering through the tree branches to see Jesus was the answer. But Jesus didn't leave him there. He told him to come down because he wanted to visit with Zacchaeus at his house.

When Jesus wanted to make a difference in Zacchaeus' life, he did it by spending time with him. Jesus wants to make a difference in your life, too, but he needs to spend time with you to do it. When you read God's word and pray, you're hanging out with Jesus and letting his words change you. Like Zacchaeus, the more you spend time with God, the more you'll learn to love and obey him. When Jesus left that day, Zacchaeus' life was changed. He showed that by returning all he'd stolen times four and giving half of what he owned to the poor. Are you letting Jesus spend time with you so your life can be changed too?

Dear Jesus, thank you for wanting to spend time with me. Help that time with you to change me—to make me into the person you want me to be. Amen.

Spring Training

Train yourself to be godly. For physical training is of
some value, but godliness has value for all things, holding
promise for both the present life and the life to come.

I TIMOTHY 4:7B-8

Have you ever watched a football team practice? They don't just toss the ball from person to person for a few minutes, then quit. The exercise is intense—they race, run drills, and sweat by what seems like the gallon—and that's only for spring training.

You're in training, too, but not the football kind. God says you're training in godliness—learning how to be like him. Like an athlete, your training doesn't start one day and end the next. If you let yourself slack off, you'll lose some of your spiritual muscle. That means you need to exercise your spiritual disciplines everyday if you can: reading the Bible, praying, and hanging out with other Christians. All of these things help you become more godly, but the most important part is your heart. Why are you training? Is it to show others how godly you're becoming, or is it to honor God? Keep practicing and keep training—not for yourself but for Jesus.

Dear God, thank you for making me more like you every day. Help me practice my spiritual disciplines so that I can know you better. Help me to be godly. In Jesus' name, amen.

No Strain At All

There you saw how The Lord your God carried you, as a
father carries his son, all The way you went until you
reached This place.

DEUTERONOMY 1:31B

Have you ever watched a dad carry a child on his shoulders? He picks him up, swings him around, and lifts him to the sky with almost no strain at all. He delights in carrying his son—his child is not a burden.

Maybe you don't have an earthly father who carried you, but God carries you. You're not a burden to him—he wants to bring you through whatever problem you're having. Over and over again in the Bible, God refers to himself as a father—your father. No matter how big you get, you'll always need your daddy. He's not only your Heavenly Father, he's also God—so his power has no limit.

Feeling weighed down today? Your parents aren't getting along again? Your locker wouldn't open? Your crush doesn't like you back? Your cell phone got dumped in the toilet? Tell your Father how you feel. Let him pick you up and let him carry you through. Really—it's no strain at all.

Dear God, thank you for being my Heavenly Father. Help me remember to bring my problems to you. I know there's nothing too big or too small for you to handle. Amen.

You'll Have Enough

Then he took the seven loaves and the fish, and when he had given thanks, he broke them and gave them to the disciples, and they in turn to the people. They all ate and were satisfied. Afterward the disciples picked up seven basketfuls of broken pieces that were left over.

MATTHEW 15:36–37

Have you ever been afraid that you would run out of something? It could be food, a place to live, or it could be as simple as having enough time in the day to finish your homework.

Jesus has compassion for people who worry that they won't have enough. One day he was teaching a crowd of people and he began to feel sorry for them because they had been there three days, and their food was gone. He told the disciples to bring him seven loaves of bread and a few small fish. His followers didn't think it would be enough, but Jesus in his great power, multiplied the food, and fed over four thousand people with it. In the end, there were seven baskets of food left over.

Jesus will never let you go without what you need. He has more than you could ask for, and wants to show you that he can powerfully provide in your life. How has Jesus provided for you?

Are you worried about having enough? Or is there someone you know who doesn't have enough of something? Ask God to provide for you or for that person—he might even want to use you to help meet the needs of someone else.

Stand Strong

Then one of The Twelve—The one called Judas Iscariot—went To The chief priests and asked, "What are you willing To give me if I deliver him over To you?" So They counted out for him Thirty pieces of silver.

MATTHEW 26:14-15

Has anyone ever made fun of you for believing in Jesus? Maybe they didn't understand why you go to church, why you use good language, or why you have a positive attitude. Your friends might think you're just trying to show off to make them feel bad. They might not understand that you're doing all these things because you love Jesus.

Sometimes it can be tempting to hide the fact that you're a Christian—to betray who you believe in. Judas Iscariot, one of Jesus' followers, told Jesus' enemies where he was so they could kill him. They gave Judas thirty pieces of silver, but Judas immediately felt guilty. Jesus' eleven other followers also ran away in fear the night before he was crucified. They didn't have the Holy Spirit in them yet, to help them stand strong and say they believed in Jesus.

You do have the Holy Spirit in you, and he empowers you to say yes to following Jesus even when others make fun of you. Next time you feel tempted to give in because others don't understand, ask Jesus for strength to stand strong in your beliefs.

Dear Jesus, help me to stand strong for you. Help me to obey you even when it's not the popular thing to do. I love you. Amen.

The Unlovables

A man wiTh Leprosy came To him and begged him on his knees, "If
you are wilLing, you can make me cLean."

MARK 1:40

Is there someone at your school that no one seems to like? Maybe they look different, talk different, or smell different. Maybe people talk about them or even do imitations of them. You feel sorry for that person, but you're not sure that you want to get involved. What if people start making fun of you too?

In Jesus' day, people were afraid of lepers—people with leprosy. Leprosy is a painful disease that disfigures the skin and nerves of those who have it. People in Bible times were so afraid of getting leprosy that sick groups of people had to live separately from everyone else. The moment a person came down with leprosy, they had to move away from everyone they loved. Jesus wasn't afraid to go to where they lived, though. He knew the risks, but he loved them anyway.

Is there someone your age in your church or school who needs you to love them? Could you ask them if they want a hug? Could you hang out with them? Could you be a friend to them? You can be like Jesus by loving the people no one else will.

Dear Jesus, help me love the people no one else loves. Help me to be like you—willing to spend time with others who are lonely and hurting. I know you can give me your love and kindness for everyone. In Jesus' name, amen.

Why Are You Going?

Jesus entered The Temple courts and drove out all who were buying and selling There. He overturned The Tables of The money changers and The benches of Those selling doves. "IT is written," he said To Them, "'My house will be called a house of prayer,' but you are making iT 'a den of robbers.'"

MATTHEW 21:12-13

Do you go to church to focus on God or something else? Do you go to see your crush, or to worship? Do you go to receive something, or to give something?

Jesus was angry when he entered the temple—the place of worship—one day. He noticed some people had set up storefronts where churchgoers could buy the sacrifices they would offer to God. Instead of people coming to church to pray, people were there to make money. In his frustration, Jesus knocked down all the tables of the storekeepers, and they ran from the building.

What's your focus? Is there anything keeping you from worshiping God at church? It isn't supposed to be about you—the clothes you wear, the offering you bring, or the talents you use. Go to church with a serious mentality—one that wants to worship God. He sees your attitude, and he's honored when you make it all about him.

Dear God, help me go to church thinking about you. Help me to remember that worshiping you is serious, and I should always think about what I can bring instead of what I can get. I love you. Amen.

Out in the Cold

While they were there, the time came for the baby to be born, and she gave birth to her firstborn, a son. She wrapped him in cloths and placed him in a manger, because there was no guest room available for them.

LUKE 2:6–7

When's the last time you felt left out? Maybe you're the youngest in your family and it feels like you don't get to do as much. Maybe you didn't get an invitation to a party you'd been waiting for. Maybe everyone else made the basketball team, but your name wasn't on the list.

Jesus understands how it feels to be left out. From the day he was born, he didn't fit in—his mother and father couldn't even find a room where he could be born. He was placed in a dirty animal feeder in a filthy barn. He was raised in a small town as the son of a humble carpenter. From the outside, Jesus didn't belong anywhere. But God had a special plan for his life.

God has a special plan for your life. You were put on this earth to do something amazing. So next time you feel left out, just remember that even Jesus probably felt that way sometimes. Because he's with you, you're never left out.

Dear Jesus, thank you for not leaving me alone. Help me to trust that you have an amazing plan for my life, even if I sometimes feel left out. In your name, amen.

You Can Have It All

The devil Led him up To a high place and showed him in an instant all The kingdoms of The world. And he said To him, "I will give you all Their authoriTy and splendor; iT has been given To me, and I can give iT To anyone I want To. If you worship me, iT will all be yours."

LUKE 4:5–7

Did you know even Jesus was tempted sometimes? In fact, the Bible says he was tempted for forty days by Satan in the wilderness. One of the temptations he faced was when Satan offered him all the kingdoms of the world if he would worship him.

As you get older, you'll be tempted sometimes to worship money or possessions instead of Jesus. You might start having thoughts about skipping church or not reading your Bible—after all, you're super busy earning money for God. But going to church and reading your Bible are what keep you close to God. Jesus knew that all the money and kingdoms of the world weren't worth the tradeoff—and it's not worth the tradeoff for you, either. Worshiping God is the most important thing in this life.

Plan now for when temptation comes. Ask God to help you stand strong and not let money or things become most important. With his help, you can keep him at the center of your life.

Dear Jesus, thank you for showing me that I can overcome any temptation. Help me to love you most of all and always put you first. Amen.

There's a Harvest

When he saw the crowds, he had compassion on them . . . Then he said to his disciples, "The harvest is plentiful but the workers are few. Ask the Lord of the harvest, therefore, to send out workers into his harvest field."

MATTHEW 9:36a, 37–38

Did you know there are people around the world who have never heard the name of Jesus? Some might live in Asia, Australia, North America, or anywhere on earth. They might live in the city, or live in the jungle. Wherever they are, Jesus sees them and has compassion for them. He says those people are like a crop that's ready for harvest—they're just waiting and ready to hear about him, but no one is there to tell them. No one is working in the field.

You might not be old enough yet to travel and tell those people about Jesus, but there is something important you can do: you can ask Jesus to send missionaries to those people. He says your prayers are important. When you ask him, the Lord of the harvest, to send workers—he'll answer you! One day you might get to see the answer to your prayer: someone who knows Jesus because you prayed for a missionary to tell them the good news. Will you have compassion and pray for someone who needs Jesus today?

Dear Jesus, I pray for those around the world who don't know you. I pray you'll send workers into your harvest to help them. I pray that one day, if you ask me, I'll be a worker and go too. I love you. Amen.

A Little Yeast Goes a Long Way

When pride comes, Then comes disgrace, buT wiTh humiLiTy comes wisdom.

PROVERBS 11:2

When you're making pizza crust with your mom, you add a pinch of something called yeast to the dough. It has to be just the right amount of yeast, otherwise you'll have pizza dough that rises so tall it looks like a loaf of bread!

Pride is a little bit like using a lot of yeast in a recipe. If you use too much, you become prideful. Before you know it, you're acting so proud that no one can tell you what to do. Are you listening in church, or are you talking over your youth leader? Are you obeying at home, or are you explaining why your way is best? You don't want to be a know-it-all who no one wants to be around. Remember, a little bit of pride goes a long way.

Dear God, help me with my pride. I know if I'm not careful it can grow into a big problem. Help my attitude to be pleasing to you, and help me to stay humble. In Jesus' name, amen.

More Than Your Name

He calls his own sheep by name and leads them out.
JOHN 10:3B

Have you ever met a set of identical twins? These two people might've talked, laughed, or even dressed the same. As hard as you tried, it might've been difficult to tell who was who. What if you tried to call one twin by name but you got it wrong?

Jesus says he knows exactly who you are, and as one of his followers, he calls you by name. He'll never confuse you with anyone else because he made you. He knows your eye color and your hair color. He knows what time you like to go to bed and what time you like to get up. He knows your favorite school subject, and which subject you wish you could skip. He knows all of it— the good and the bad—and he loves you.

Dear God, thank you for knowing me better than anyone else. You don't just know my name—you know and love all of me. Help me to follow you. In Jesus' name, amen.

DAY 154

Searching for It

BLessed are Those who find wisdom, Those who gain understanding, for she is more profiTable Than silver and yields better returns Than gold.

PROVERBS 3:13-14

Have you ever had a crush on someone? Maybe you wrote notes to them, or made excuses to be in the same place at the same time. Maybe you invited your crush to your soccer game, or the play you were in. You wanted to be close to that person—they were on your mind all the time.

God says wisdom is a lot like a person you have a crush on. When you pursue wisdom, you look for it in the Bible every day. You think about it all the time. You ask God to show you how to do the right thing in each situation in your life. You can even find wisdom by reading this devotional! The index in the back of the book is a great place to start—it will tell you which pages share which verses about almost every situation you will face.

Pursue wisdom. Think about it constantly, and it will reward you for the rest of your life.

Dear God, I want to search for wisdom. Please give me a desire to pursue it. Thank you for promising me that it will reward me when I look for it in your word. In Jesus' name, amen.

DAY 155

The Master Calendar

Instead, you ought to say, "If it is the Lord's will, we will live and do this or that."

JAMES 4:15

Isn't it a bummer when your plans with a friend don't work out? Maybe your mom says no, or the weather doesn't cooperate. It's hard not to feel disappointed when you're missing out on something fun.

The Bible says people make plans in their hearts, but the Lord directs their steps. In other words, you're not completely in control of what happens when you make a plan. Does that mean you shouldn't  put things on your calendar? Of course not! Go ahead and talk about the basketball game, or the pool party, or the youth group rally. But remember as you plan that God is the one who holds the master calendar, and has your best interest at heart. When things don't work out as you'd hoped, remember that his will—his purpose—is working in a way you might not understand yet. You can trust him when things go differently, and you can learn to say that his plan is best.

Dear God, I trust you with my plans. When things don't go as I want, you are in control and you can handle my disappointment. Thank you for having my best interest at heart. I love you. Amen.

DAY 156

No Secrets

You may be sure that your sin will find you out.
NUMBERS 32:23B

When you plan a surprise birthday party, you do everything you can to keep it a secret. There's probably a lot of whispering, planning, and promising to keep things quiet. Sometimes, though, someone may accidentally say something and the surprise is spoiled. All your planning doesn't work out.

There are other secrets in life—not just good ones—that will eventually be discovered. You might try to keep it quiet if you've cheated on a test or if you've taken something that doesn't belong to you. But God says eventually your sin will be found out—so wouldn't you rather confess now than be caught? He's always ready to forgive you when you're willing to face the consequences. No matter how hard you try, your mistake will always catch up with you.

Is there a sin in your life that you need to confess? Tell God about it, and then tell the people you've wronged. It might be embarrassing to admit you messed up, but it's better than letting someone else discover what's happened. 'Fess up and you'll feel better.

Grumpy Giving

Each of you should give what you have decided in your heart to give, not reluctantly or under compulsion, for God loves a cheerful giver.

2 Corinthians 9:7

Have you ever been tucked in cozy tight and your mom yelled for you to get up? It's hard to roll out of those warm, soft sheets when you're in the middle of a deep sleep. It's even harder when you know you're getting up because you volunteered to be somewhere you might not really want to go.

It's important to volunteer to do things for other people sometimes. God says he loves a cheerful giver, and he's not just talking about cheerfully giving money—he's talking about cheerfully giving your time. Maybe you volunteer at the soup kitchen, or the church cleanup day, or the school fundraiser. Whatever it is, you're doing something for someone else—and you get to pick the attitude you'll have when you do it. Will you be grumpy and complaining the whole time? Or will you choose to give your time cheerfully? When you choose to have a good attitude, you'll find the time passes much more quickly, and you might even discover you're having fun along the way.

Dear God, help me be a cheerful giver of my time. Help me not complain, but to be happy that I can do something for someone else. In Jesus' name, amen.

A Light for the Lost

I have come into the world as a light, so that no one who believes in me should stay in darkness.

JOHN 12:46

Did you ever get lost in a store when you were a little kid? Maybe you were hiding in a clothes rack or peeking in the candy aisle—when all of a sudden you turned around and your mom wasn't there. Do you remember the feeling of panic that came over your body? Who could you talk to? Where could you go?

The Bible says there are people in the world who are every bit as lost as you felt. They might not realize it, but they're living in the dark—without the light of Jesus to show them right from wrong. The good news is, because Jesus lives inside of you, you can be a light to those people. You can be a light to your friend when you help her practice for a basketball game, for your enemy when you forgive him for stealing your lunch, and to your teacher when you choose to study for your test. People all around you are waiting to see a difference in you. Will you be a light for Jesus today?

Dear Jesus, help me to be a light to others around me. Help me to be so different—so kind, so loving—that they want to know you because of it. In Jesus' name, amen.

Loving = Listening

If you love me, keep my commands.
JOHN 14:15

What type of house rules does your family have? Maybe it's no video games until after homework, or no texting on school nights. (Or maybe you need to fill in the blank.) Those rules are there to help you stay healthy and happy—your parents really want the very best for you.

Jesus says if you love him, you'll keep his commands—and one of his commands is obeying your parents. He's always with you, so he sees when you're letting your grades slide. He knows when you stay up all night texting your crush even though your parents want you to stay healthy by getting enough sleep. And he doesn't have to sniff around to find the stash of candy underneath your mattress. It could seem like you're getting away with fun stuff, but those rules are there to help you learn to take care of yourself. Since you love Jesus and he wants the very best for you, he asks you to keep his commands—including obeying your parents. How can you do that today?

Dear God, help me to see where I can start with keeping your commands today. You know that I love you and I want to respect you too. Amen.

Don't Grieve Him

And do not grieve the Holy Spirit of God.
EPHESIANS 4:30A

If you learned that people were spreading rumors about you at school, you'd probably feel upset. But if you found out your best friend was the one who started those rumors you'd probably feel pretty sad too.

When someone you know hurts you, it's different than when a stranger does. You might feel like you've lost something—like your friendship isn't the same. God feels that way when you don't respect him. The Bible says it "grieves" him. When you choose to do the wrong thing, it creates a distance between you and God. Things like yelling at your parents, being mean to your brother, or making fun of the new kid at school all make God sad.

It's important to confess when you've made a mistake, but it's even more important to try to respect God in the first place. What are some habits you have that might grieve God's spirit? Can you talk to him about those? How can you change your actions in the future?

Dear God, I want to be close to you—to not have any distance in our friendship. Please show me if there's something I need to change so I can be closer to you. In Jesus' name, amen.

Be Brave!

She opened it and saw the baby. He was crying, and she felt sorry for him. "This is one of the Hebrew babies," she said. Then his sister asked Pharaoh's daughter, "Shall I go and get one of the Hebrew women to nurse the baby for you?"

EXODUS 2:6-7

Have you ever had a moment when you needed to be brave? Standing up for what you believe in takes courage. It also means taking risks, even if you're scared.

Baby Moses' sister knew what it was like to have courage. When all the other Hebrew babies were being killed by their enemies, Moses' sister  decided to save her brother's life. She put him in a basket and floated him toward the enemy's princess, who was bathing in the river. When the princess opened the basket, she felt sorry for baby Moses and raised him like a son.

You might not need courage to save someone's life, but you will need courage to stand up for your faith. When others make fun of you for believing in Jesus, you can take the risk and tell them about him anyway. Courage isn't just a feeling you get—it's a decision you make. Like Moses' sister, you can come up with a plan for what to do when you need courage. Will you stand up for Jesus even when it feels risky?

Write down a few sentences about how Jesus has helped you. When the time comes, you can tell someone sincerely about the difference Jesus has made in your life.

He Won't Shoo You Away

PeopLe were bringing LiTTLe chiLdren To Jesus for him To pLace his
hands on Them, buT The discipLes rebuked Them. When Jesus saw
This, he was indignanT . . . And he Took The chiLdren in his arms,
pLaced his hands on Them and bLessed Them.

MARK 10:13–14B, 16

Have you ever been in a church service that didn't seem very interesting?
Maybe the songs had weird words, or the Bible verses were confusing.
Not much of the service seemed like it was meant for someone your age.

Sometimes adults make stuff complicated, but did you know Jesus
said that everyone needs to have simple faith like a child? When Jesus'
disciples tried to shoo some young people away from Jesus so adults
could see him instead, Jesus was upset. He hugged those children and
blessed them.

You're important to God. Even when you don't enjoy the songs or
understand the verses, you get the most important thing: you believe
what he says. So next time you're feeling overlooked, know that Jesus
thinks you have amazing faith. He loves you and knows that one day you
will change the world.

Dear Jesus, thank you for giving me amazing faith in you. Help me to
learn to be more and more like you. I love you. Amen.

Dark Magic

> So The king summoned The magicians, enchanters, sorcerers and astrologers To Tell him what he had dreamed. When They came in and stood before The king, he said To Them, "I have had a dream That Troubles me and I want To know what it means."
>
> **DANIEL 2:2-3**

When your mom's driving down the road and you see a psychic's office, do you ever wonder what it's like inside? Have you ever seen a Ouija board at a slumber party? What about those magazines in the store that promise they'll predict your future?

There are people everywhere who say they know what will happen in your life. King Nebuchadnezzar had an entire team of astrologers (people

who claimed to read the stars to tell the future) and magicians who lived in his house. But magicians and astrologers aren't from God—they're from Satan. In the end, only God could help Nebuchadnezzar.

God is the only one who can help you too. Don't fall for tricks and distractions. Next time you're tempted to have your palm read or look up astrology signs, know that those things aren't the same as asking God for advice. You might not know your future—but you know the one who planned it, and you can trust him with it.

Make a plan of action for the next time your friends are playing with a Ouija board or looking at their astrological signs. Are you willing to kindly tell them you can't be a part of that?

You're More Than Okay

BuT we have This Treasure in jars of cLay To show ThaT This aLL-
surpassing power is from God and noT from us.
2 CORINTHIANS 4:7

Have you ever met someone who really understood you? Maybe they'd been through similar problems as you have. They might be having trouble with homework or their siblings. You were able to talk about your problems and you both felt understood.

God says it's okay that you're not perfect. In fact, he says he made you that way on purpose. In 2 Corinthians, Paul compares your body to a clay jar—you're a little broken in some places. That might mean you struggle in music class, or that your hands shake when you have to give a speech. It might mean you fumble the ball, or you just can't remember the concepts in geometry. Whatever your struggles are, other people see them and can relate to you. They don't need to see another "perfect" person—they need to see someone who relies on God's strength in their weaknesses. So next time you feel like life just isn't lining up for you, remember it's okay—God has this, and his power will see you through.

Dear God, thank you for not needing me to be perfect. Thank you for working in the middle of my struggles, and that those struggles can help others see you. Help me to rely on you for my strength. In Jesus' name, amen.

Will You Carry Them?

They gathered in such large numbers that there was no room left, not even outside the door, and he preached the word to them. Some men came, bringing to him a paralyzed man, carried by four of them.

MARK 2:2–3

When Jesus first started his ministry, people came from long distances to hear him preach. The crowds were so large that it was hard to get close. One paralyzed man had friends who knew Jesus could heal him—if only they could get Jesus' attention. Since they couldn't reach Jesus, they made a hole in the roof of the house where Jesus was teaching and lowered their friend down to him. That was determination!

How determined are you to help your friends who need Jesus? When one of them is struggling, do you pray for them? Sometimes when a friend is having a hard time, it's tough for them to have faith in God. Like the paralyzed man, they feel stuck in their situation. Who can you pray for today?

Make a list of people who might not have faith in Jesus. Every day after you read your devotional, pray for those friends.

Not a Counterfeit

These people honor me with their lips, but their hearts are far from me. They worship me in vain; their teachings are merely human rules.

MARK 7:6B–7

What if someone gave you $100 for your birthday? Would you be surprised? Would you think and plan before you shopped for what you wanted? What if you went to pay for your present, but the cashier told you the money wasn't real—it was counterfeit? How would that make you feel?

There is such a thing as being a counterfeit Christian too. Jesus said there are some people who follow all the rules—read the Bible—go to church—but their hearts aren't in it. The church leaders of his day knew how to make rules, and were good at following them—but underneath their hearts didn't love God. Take a minute to think and pray. It's easy to get caught up in the motions of going to church and reading your devotional. But is your heart in it? If it isn't, what can you do to change that? God loves you, and he doesn't want you to have to be a counterfeit Christian.

Dear God, help me to be sincere in my love for you. Help me to be the real deal—to go to church and read my Bible not just because I have to, but because I love you. In Jesus' name, amen.

Where Are You Looking?

Then Peter got down out of the boat, walked on the water and came toward Jesus. But when he saw the wind, he was afraid and, beginning to sink, cried out, "Lord, save me!" Immediately Jesus reached out his hand and caught him. "You of little faith," he said, "why did you doubt?"

MATTHEW 14:29B–31

Have you ever faced a problem so big that it was hard to trust God? Sometimes people you love get sick, you lose a pet, or you're bullied at school. Life hurts, and in the middle of your problems it's hard to remember God's in control.

After Jesus miraculously calmed the storm that was tossing the disciples' boat, Peter asked if he could walk on the water with him. Peter took one step—then two—then he looked around, got worried, and began to sink. He called to Jesus for help and Jesus saved him.

Peter's eyes were on his problems instead of Jesus. When we look at our problems like Peter, we begin to get overwhelmed. Instead of focusing on what's hurting right now, can you focus on how Jesus can help you? If you're feeling like life's just too hard, call out to Jesus. He's waiting to catch you—he'll never let you fall.

Dear Jesus, on days when I feel overwhelmed, help me to keep my focus on you. I know that you're powerful and you can bring me through the hard times. I love you. Amen.

Streets of Gold?

The great street of the city was of gold, as pure as transparent glass.

REVELATION 21:21b

Can you imagine if you walked out the front door of your house and discovered the street was paved with gold? Word would probably spread fast and people would dig holes until the entire street was gone.

The Bible says heaven is so amazing that there's a street of gold. The gates are made of pearls, and everyone who believes in Jesus will have a home he's thoughtfully prepared for them. We're not sure if the Bible means there will be a literal street of gold and gates of pearls—but we do know that Jesus is preparing a home for us that's beyond our wildest dreams. Best of all, he promises there won't be any more crying, no more death—no more sadness. Jesus will wipe away every tear from your eyes.

We don't know all the details of heaven, but we know it's more amazing than anything we've ever experienced. If you've never told Jesus you want to spend forever in heaven with him some day, you can do that today. It's as easy as 1–2–3: 1) Tell God you've sinned. 2) Tell him you believe Jesus died to take the punishment for your sin. 3) Tell him you want to live your life for him. He wants to prepare a home especially for you.

Dear God, I know that I'm a sinner. I choose to believe that Jesus died to forgive my sin. I want to live making right choices for you. Thank you for preparing a place for me in my forever home. Amen.

Never Beyond God's Reach

When he came To JerusaLem, he Tried To join The disciples, buT
They were all afraid of him, noT believing ThaT he really was a
disciple. BuT Barnabas Took him and broughT him To The apostles.

ACTS 9:26–27A

Who's the meanest person you know? Is it a bully at school? Is it some-one in your family? Is it someone on the other team? Did you know Jesus loves that person?

There was a man in the Bible named Saul who was the enemy of every Christian. He hated Christians so much that he gathered everyone he could find and killed them. The people were terrified, but then one day

Jesus appeared to Saul in a vision. That day, Saul put his trust in Jesus and his life was completely changed. At first, other Christians thought he was pretending so he could capture them. They didn't trust him. But soon they realized he really *was* changed—Jesus' love had reached even their worst enemy.

Can you think of the person you dislike most? Will you pray for that person? It might be that Jesus wants to use you to show his love in their life. Your prayers are powerful, and you might get to see God transform even your worst enemy.

Make a list of the people in your life who are hard to love. Add them to your devotional book and pray for them. In praying for them, you might feel your heart growing in love for that person.

Body Boundaries

But among you There must not be even a hint of sexual immoraliTy, or any kind of impuriTy, or of greed, because These are improper for God's holy peopLe.

EPHESIANS 5:3

Do your parents have rules about dating? Are you allowed to have a boyfriend or a girlfriend? Whether you're waiting to date or you're already hanging out with your crush, you should set some physical boundaries for yourself.

Your body is your body—it doesn't belong to anyone else. You should never feel pressured by anyone to do something you don't want to do and that doesn't honor God. God says there shouldn't be even a hint of impurity—that means you should follow his rules about romantic relationships. Talk with your parents—when is it okay for you to hold hands with someone? Hug? Only you, God, and your parents can decide what your boundaries are—but those boundaries are there to keep you safe. In the process, you'll show others that Jesus is helping you honor him with your body.

Ask your parents to sit down and write a list of things that are safe to do with your body. Put that list in a place where you'll see it often—maybe on your bathroom mirror or bedroom door. Choose to keep your body safe by following your boundaries.

Be a Barnabas

Joseph, a Levite from Cyprus, whom the apostles called Barnabas (which means "son of encouragement").

ACTS 4:36

If you had to pick up everything and move to a new town, how do you think your old friends would remember you? Would they say you were a positive person? That you loved others? That you stood up for people who couldn't stand up for themselves?

Barnabas lived in Bible times. It was a funny name—but it had a very simple meaning: "son of encouragement." Everyone who knew Barnabas knew they could count on him for a positive word in hard times. Are you a son or daughter of encouragement? When someone says something negative about someone, do you join in? Or do you stand up for that person? When someone you know is going through a rough spot, do you reach out and listen to their problems? You can become a son or daughter of encouragement just by being a caring person. Is there someone you can encourage today?

Think about someone in your life who's struggling. Give them a call or text to see how they're doing. They need someone to listen and care. You can be that person.

You're Not Powerless

"Pardon me, my Lord," Gideon replied, "but how can I save Israel? My clan is the weakest in Manasseh, and I am the Least in my family."
JUDGES 6:15

Is there someone who picks on you at school? Maybe it's just "poking fun" or maybe it's more serious than that (if it is, you should definitely talk to an adult about what's happening). Sometimes it's hard to know what to do when you feel powerless against a bully.

The people of Israel were being bullied by a nation called Midian. When God wanted Israel to stand up for itself, he chose a man named Gideon to lead the cause. But Gideon was reluctant. He knew his family was small and no one really knew him. How could he convince anyone to defend themselves against the Midianites? Again and again, God promised Gideon he would be with him, and in the end Gideon led 300 men to victory over the huge Midianite army.

God is on your side. No matter how small you feel, you can believe in yourself. That might mean telling your bully to lay off, or it might mean reaching out to an adult for help. God loves you, and like Gideon, he can help you overcome the bullies in your life.

Dear God, I'm tired of being bullied. Help me to know what to do. Like you did with Gideon, you can use someone who feels powerless to overcome bullies. In Jesus' name, amen.

Even If . . . God is Still Good

If we are thrown into the blazing furnace, the God we serve
is able to deliver us from it, and he will deliver us from your
Majesty's hand. But even if he does not, we want you to know,
your Majesty, that we will not serve your gods.

DANIEL 3:17–18A

Wouldn't it be nice if God always rushed in and rescued you from your problems? There were three men in the Bible who had a huge problem—they were told they would be killed because they refused to worship the king. Before they were thrown into a blazing fire as a penalty, one of them told the king: "The God we serve is able to deliver us from it . . . but even if he does not . . ."

Even when bad or scary things happen, God is still good. He isn't good because of what he does for you—he's good because of who he is. Oftentimes God will rescue you, just like he rescued the men who chose to worship him instead of the king. But even when he doesn't—you can still thank him. He loves you, and he is good.

Dear God, sometimes it's hard to trust everything will work out. But I believe that even in the middle of my problems you're still there. Thank you for seeing and understanding more than I do. In Jesus' name, amen.

Never Begging Bread

I was young and now I am old, yet I have never seen the righteous forsaken or their children begging bread.

PSALM 37:25

Sometimes you might hear your parents talking about bills, groceries, or what they wish they had. Maybe you worry that there's not enough money to go around, or maybe you even know what it's like to go without something you need.

God wants you to know you're not alone. He promises that when you have a need—a true need—he's going to take care of it. Sometimes there are things in life you might want, like a new outfit, a new bike, or a new game—but those things are wants, not needs. God knows what you need: food, shelter, and someone to love you. God's power is unlimited, and he's ready to meet your needs when you ask him. He'll never let you go without.

Do you have a need you can talk to God about? If not, do you have a friend who has a need? You can trust God to provide for you, or you can be the one to help provide for a friend who is going without.

Don't Throw a Fit

BuT godLiness wiTh conTenTmenT is greaT gain.

I TIMOTHY 6:6

Have you ever watched a toddler stomp his foot? Maybe he threw himself on the ground, screaming and crying, trying to get what he wanted. If a parent always gives in to a toddler, the child will learn he gets what he wants just by throwing a fit. Most parents know they can't give their kids everything they want—some things toddlers ask for are dangerous or unhealthy.

God knows there are some things that are dangerous or unhealthy for you to have too. You might have asked him again and again for something but the answer seemed to be "no." You might really want to make the team, but God has something better in store for you. You might really want a new skateboard, but God wants you to learn to be content with the bike you have. Or you might have asked him for an amazing best friend, but the right person hasn't come along yet.

If you're asking God for something and his answer is no, don't be discouraged. He's watching out for you and he wants the very best for you, because you're his child.

Dear God, thank you for watching out for me and teaching me to be content. I trust that when I want something, you know exactly what I *need*—even when it's not exactly what I had in mind. In Jesus' name, amen.

DAY 176

How Do We Know the Bible is True?

Jesus Took The Twelve aside and Told Them, "We are going up To Jerusalem, and everything That is written by The prophets about The Son of Man will be fulfilled."
LUKE 18:31

How do we know the Bible is true? After all, there's a story about a boat that saved animals and people from a world-wide flood. Also, there's one about a man who was swallowed by a fish. And what about the time Jesus walked on water?

One of the ways we can know the Bible is true is because it contains prophecies. That means that people of God wrote down everything he told them would happen—and thousands of years later, those things did happen. One of those many prophecies was that Jesus would come to earth, die for our sins, and be raised to life three days later. Those predictions came true. Only God knows the future, and it's one of the many reasons we can trust his word today.

What are some other ways you can know the Bible is true? Ask your youth leader or a Christian adult and make a list. Also, keep reading this devotional because we'll discuss even more reasons soon.

What's Discernment?

Nor should There be obscenity, foolish Talk or coarse joking,
which are out of place, but rather Thanksgiving.
EPHESIANS 5:4

What's the most difficult muscle in your whole body to control? Your tongue! When you have a thought about something or someone, do you think about how what you're going to say is going to make someone else feel?

Not saying everything you think is showing self-control. The Bible says we shouldn't talk about things that are obscene (like something bad someone might tell you was in an R-rated movie), or foolish (like making fun of someone), or joking (the kind of jokes that your friends might call "dirty"). In a Christian's life, God says those things are completely out of place. Instead, think of something positive and thank God for it.

Next time you have a thought you know you shouldn't share, take a minute and think. You can replace that thought with good things and control that little muscle called your tongue.

Make a list of things you can thank God for next time bad thoughts enter your mind. Add to that list over time as you think of more things. You can be a positive person just by learning to control your tongue.

Don't Be a Couch Potato

For even when we were with you, we gave you this rule: "The one who is unwilling to work shall not eat."
2 Thessalonians 3:10

It's possible to let others do all the work without realizing it. It's pretty easy to get caught up in what you need to do—your homework, your ball games, and your extracurricular activities—and not pay attention to what others are doing. If you don't have assigned chores, you might not notice how much other people are doing around the house. In the Bible, Paul made a rule for Jesus' followers: if they didn't work, they didn't get to eat. What if that was a rule in your house?

Look around you today and ask your family the question, "How can I help?" They might be surprised, but they'll be grateful for the assistance. Don't be a couch potato. You can be a contributing part of your family, and they'll thank you.

Dear God, help me notice people around me and help them. I don't want to always let everyone else do all the work—I want to be a part of what's going on in my family. In Jesus' name, amen.

Being in Charge

Now the overseer is to be above reproach, faithful to his wife, temperate, self-controlled, respectable, hospitable, able to teach.
1 Timothy 3:2

Do you want to be a leader? It might look like it's fun to be on the stage at your church, or up front teaching in the younger kids' classes. But did you know that God holds leaders to a higher standard? If you want to lead, you need to know how to set a good example for the people you're leading.

The apostle Paul gave us examples of what church leaders should be: good examples, faithful, gentle, self-controlled, respected, giving, and educated in the Bible well enough to teach. You're not an adult yet, so you have time to practice all these good qualities. Are you setting a good example with your language? Are you practicing self-control? Are you thinking of thoughtful things you can do for your family? Are you learning your Bible well enough to teach someone else?

This world needs good leaders. It might feel like a lot of responsibility to learn all the qualities Paul mentioned, but you'll get there. Pick one quality you can work on today, and you'll be on your way to being the leader God wants you to be.

Write down the list of qualities Paul listed for being a good leader. Now circle the one you think needs the most work. See if you can find an adult to help you become better at the things you need to be!

Strengthening Faith

He has delivered us from such a deadly peril, and he will deliver us again. On him we have set our hope that he will continue to deliver us.

2 Corinthians 1:10

You can see God's faithfulness in your life every day. Every time he gives you breath, that's his faithfulness. Every time he helps you through a tough situation with your parents, that's his faithfulness. Every time he helps you to be kind to your arch-nemesis, that's his faithfulness too.

But do you know what else will show you God's faithfulness? Hearing the stories about others God has rescued. If you haven't taken a look at the heroes of the Bible, you can find a list of amazing ones in Hebrews 11. If your church has a library, or if it's okay with your parents, do an Internet search for Christian heroes. Their stories will amaze you. Many of these heroes faced imprisonment, separation from their families, and even death—all while staying strong in their faith.

If you're looking for a place to start, look up the names Mary Slessor, Katie Davis, or Hudson Taylor. You can also ask your parents or other Christians how God has been faithful to them. Their lives will inspire you to look to God for your strength, and to recognize how good he's been to you.

Thank you, Jesus, that you are faithful to me. Thank you for the heroes who have gone before me and who can teach me more about trusting you. Help me to be inspired by your faithfulness. In Jesus' name, amen.

DAY 181

Fresh Food

The people of Israel called the bread manna. It was white like coriander seed and tasted like wafers made with honey.

EXODUS 16:31

If you want to keep your food fresh, where do you store it? The refrigerator or the dinner table? When God's people were traveling through the desert, the weather was hot and dry—there was no place to keep their food cool. So every day, God sent them bread called manna. It was exactly what they needed when they needed it.

God's Word, the Bible, is exactly what you need when you need it. It's a lot like that manna—you need a fresh supply every day. That's why there are 365 days in this devotional; something new for each day of the year. God knows exactly what words you need to read today, tomorrow, and the next day. It's okay if you miss a day here or there, but it's hard to live on leftovers forever. Try to hear from him every day and it will be just what you need.

If you aren't already, try to put a bookmark on the day you last read in your devotional. That way it's easy to get to just the right spot to find the spiritual food you need for tomorrow.

Learn From My Mistakes

These Things happened To Them as examples and were written down as warnings for us, on whom The culmination of The ages has come.

1 CORINTHIANS 10:11

If you've ever been rock climbing, you know there's an advantage to not being first on the mountainside. Usually the most experienced climber goes first—it's that person's job to scout out the trouble spots, warn those below, and give instructions for climbing. The first climber makes the climb a lot easier for the rest of the climbers.

The Bible was written—hundreds of pages over thousands of years—so that we could learn from the mistakes of those who went before us. We see selfishness, greed, envy, and every wrong action laid out in its pages. We also see the consequences of those actions.

You can avoid making the same mistakes of people who lived before you. Study the Bible. Learn from its characters. Sin started with the people of the Bible, and you can learn to steer clear of the rough patches where they stumbled. By studying God's Word, you can climb high without getting injured.

Can you name two characters in the Bible who made mistakes you want to avoid? Why don't you write down their names? What were the mistakes they made, and how can you learn from them?

Truth in Action

Dear children, Let us not Love with words or speech but with actions and in Truth.

I John 3:18

Have you ever looked out the window of your school bus and noticed a homeless person standing on the corner of the street? They may have been holding a sign that said, "Will work for food." What if your bus driver had cracked open his window and told the person, "I wish you all the best today! I hope you get some food!" It would have been a nice wish, but it wouldn't actually have done anything to help the person.

When someone has a need you can help with, but you don't do anything about it, you're just making an empty wish for them. You shouldn't just tell them you hope things get better (although that's a great start). Think about ways you *can* help them. Maybe they're struggling with grades—can you help them study? Maybe they're struggling with parents who argue—can you invite them over for a break sometime? Or maybe they're struggling with bullies at school—can you stand up for them?

You don't just have to wish things were better for your friends. You can actually help make them better. Do you have a friend you can help today?

Dear God, help me to notice little ways to help friends who are in need. Thank you for noticing my needs and meeting them, so I can do the same for others. In Jesus' name, amen.

Taking the High Road

Do not be overcome by evil, but overcome evil with good.
ROMANS 12:21

Joseph's brothers had always been jealous of him—they knew he was their father's favorite, and they sold him into slavery because of it (Genesis 37, 39–50). After that, his life was hard. He even spent time in jail for a crime he didn't commit. He could have sulked, pouted, or even plotted revenge against his brothers. Years later when Joseph became a powerful ruler, he even had the chance to punish his brothers. Instead, he wept and forgave them.

You're going to have opportunities in life to retaliate when people hurt you. In fact, that might be the first idea that will come to you—revenge. When someone wrongs you, it might be tempting to sulk, pout, or retaliate. But God says evil isn't overcome with evil—it's only overcome with good. Can you take the high road and forgive others when they hurt you? How can you overcome evil with good today?

It's okay to feel sad when someone hurts you, but it's not okay to retaliate with the same unkindness they've shown you. Is there someone in your life you can choose to forgive? Ask God to help you. It's his strength that can bring you to a place of healing.

He Understands

Jesus wept.
JOHN 11:35

Jesus was very busy when someone came to tell him that his friend, Lazarus, was sick. He didn't seem to be in a hurry to get to Lazarus's house—he made several stops along the way. When he got there, Lazarus's sister came out to tell him that his friend was already dead.

He wasn't surprised by Lazarus's death—God's son can't be surprised. But the Bible says Jesus was so brokenhearted that he wept. Even though he knew he would raise Lazarus back to life, he felt a deep loss for his friend.

If you've lost someone you love, Jesus understands how you feel. One day he will bring your loved one back to life, but until then his heart hurts with you. He knows exactly how you feel and wants to comfort you.

Dear Jesus, thank you for becoming human so you could understand my pain. Please give me comfort when I'm missing the one I love. Death can't separate us forever—one day you'll bring my loved one back to me. Amen.

Hitting Pause

So after they had fasted and prayed, they placed their hands on them and sent them off.

ACTS 13:3

Have you ever heard the word "fasting?" It has the word "fast" in it, but it actually has to do with slowing down and focusing on prayer. Fasting means to pause on something like food, video games, or plans with friends for a time so you can give all your attention to praying.

The Bible shows us again and again how people who fasted and prayed saw God move in big ways. One of those times was when Paul and Barnabas fasted from food and prayed that God would bring a lot of people into his family. God answered their prayers, and many, many people were saved.

You can fast and pray, too, as long as it's okay with your parents. What can you pause from so you can spend more time with God?

Is there someone you know who needs prayer? Maybe someone who's sick or needs to know Jesus. Is there an activity you can give up for a day, so you can spend time praying for that person?

Wolves in Sheep's Clothing

If anyone comes to you and does not bring this teaching, do not take them into your house or welcome them.

2 John 10:10

Have you ever dressed up for a holiday or a costume party? Maybe when you got to the event you tried to guess which friend was which, but you couldn't tell because they had masks and elaborate costumes.

The Bible warns that there are people who show up at church like wolves in sheep's clothing. Of course, the Bible isn't talking about a costume party. It is saying sometimes people look like Christians but don't believe in or live what the Bible says. God makes it very clear that Jesus is the only way to be saved—that anyone who believes that he died and rose again is a true believer. The apostle Paul warned Christians that they shouldn't welcome or believe leaders who didn't teach this truth—that these people were only dressed like Christians on the outside.

Church should be a safe place where Christians go to worship, and you should always feel comfortable there. But it's a good idea to listen carefully to the beliefs of the people who are teaching you. If they don't line up with the truths of the Bible, you should talk and pray about it with your parents.

Does your church believe the Bible is true? If not, can you talk about this with your parents? They can help you decide what you need to do if others aren't teaching God's truth.

DAY 188

God's Testing

Truly I tell you, if you have faith as small as a mustard seed, you can say to this mountain, 'Move from here to there,' and it will move. Nothing will be impossible for you."

MATTHEW 17:20B

Did you know there are places outside of school that involve testing? The tough things in our lives—moving away from friends, hurtful friendships, parents divorcing—are just a few of the tests God can use to make us stronger in our faith. Like a muscle, when your faith is tested, it gets stronger and stronger.

The tests God allows in our lives strengthen our spiritual muscles. Daily challenges as well as catastrophic events are all things that can make or break our faith in God.

When things get tough, will you give up? Or will you look at it as a test that's strengthening your spiritual muscles? It doesn't take much faith for God to show you he's there—even faith as a tiny mustard seed. Will you trust him to grow your faith?

Dear God, help me to have faith to see that you're strengthening my spiritual muscles in these hard times. Help me to know that the stronger my faith in you, the better my relationship with you will be. Thank you for being with me when I'm tested. Amen.

Running the Other Way

But Jonah ran away from The Lord and headed for Tarshish. He went down to Joppa, where he found a ship bound for that port. After paying the fare, he went aboard and sailed for Tarshish to flee from The Lord.

JONAH 1:3

You may have heard the story of Jonah—the man who was too scared to be a missionary to a group of people called the Ninevites. It was understandable that Jonah was frightened when God told him to go there—the people of Nineveh were known for capturing their enemies and torturing them. When Jonah got on a boat going in the opposite direction, he ended up spending three days and three nights praying in the belly of a huge fish. Finally, the fish spit Jonah out, and he went straight to Nineveh, where the people treated him well and welcomed God into their lives.

Did you know that once you've asked Jesus to be your savior, he won't let you walk in disobedience? You can run away from what he wants you to do, but it will be very uncomfortable. You'll probably never be swallowed by a fish, but there will be consequences for your sin. If you keep doing the wrong things—lying, cheating, or bullying, for example—you're going to get in trouble with those around you. God loves you too much to let you live in disobedience.

Dear God, thank you for loving me enough to give me consequences when I disobey. Help me to honor you in everything I do, and to trust that you have good plans for me. Amen.

Hang Out with Him?

After This, Jesus went out and saw a Tax collector by The name of Levi sitting at his Tax booth. "Follow me," Jesus said To him.
LUKE 5:27

Everywhere Jesus went people were drawn to him. He loved everyone he met—healthy and sick, rich and poor, happy and sad. One day he called a tax collector to follow him (tax collectors back then often charged people too much and kept the extra for themselves). It really bothered some of the religious people that Jesus wanted to hang out with others they didn't think were good enough.

When you look at your life, who's in it? Only people who have perfect teeth, clear skin, and a cool wardrobe? Or are there some oddballs in there—people who don't quite fit in? Are you afraid to spend time with someone who's unpopular because it might ruin your social status?

Can you pick at least one person to invite over or to sit with at lunch who you normally wouldn't? There's no better way to be like Jesus than to love everyone you meet.

Dear God, even when it's hard, help me welcome others who might be different from me. Help me to see beyond what they look or act like, and love them as you loved others. Amen.

I Don't Have Much

ALL These peopLe gave Their gifTs ouT of Their weaLTh; buT she ouT of her poverTy puT in aLL She had To Live on.
LUKE 21:4

Do you ever feel like you don't have much to offer God? Maybe your wallet's not full of cash to share. Maybe you're not an athlete who can be an example by praying before games. Maybe you're not a singer who could lead a worship service. What can you do?

When Jesus was in the church one day, his followers were excited about all the money the wealthy people were putting in the offering box. Then a poor widow came and put in two small coins. They clinked in the box unimpressively—but Jesus said that her offering was more important than anyone else's had been. Others had given a portion of their wealth—but this lady gave everything she had.

When you put your heart into loving others, your offering is bigger than any talent you may or may not have. God doesn't want what you can do for him as much as he wants your whole heart. You can make a huge difference when you give him your all.

Dear God, I give you all of myself. I want to love others with everything I have—no matter how much talent I have or I don't have. I know you can use anyone who is fully devoted to you. I love you. Amen.

Music in Prison

Give Thanks in all circumstances; for This is God's will for you in Christ Jesus.

I Thessalonians 5:18

Johann Sebastian Bach was one of the greatest composers of all times. In fact, he was such an amazing musician that when he tried to quit his job playing music for the duke, he put Bach in prison. But that didn't stop Bach. While he was in prison he wrote many of his greatest pieces—songs musicians around the world still play almost 300 years later.

Sometimes it's going to seem like you're imprisoned by problems in your life. Maybe your school's tough, your health's bad, or your family situation isn't working out so well. You might feel stuck. But try to remember, you can do great things even when you can't change your circumstances. When he was imprisoned, the apostle Paul wrote letters to people around the world—letters in the Bible we still live by today

You're never completely stuck in your situation. You can choose to give thanks to God that he's with you in it and will help bring purpose out of your pain.

Do you have a journal? Sometimes writing helps free you when you feel imprisoned in your problems. All you need is some paper and a pen or pencil. If you have time, you can start one right now!

The Very Rich Man

Jesus looked at them and said, "With man this is impossible, but not with God; all things are possible with God."

MARK 10:27

Jesus was on a long dusty road when he met a very rich man. The man told Jesus that he loved God a lot and wanted to please him. He listed all the good things he'd done, and Jesus asked him if he would be willing to give up the things he owned to show he loved God most. The Bible says the man walked away very sad.

At some point, Jesus might ask you to give up something important. It might be a boyfriend or girlfriend that's not a Christian, a bad habit, or some of your possessions. He won't ask you to give those things up so you'll be miserable—he'll ask you so that you know in your heart that *he* has first place. Giving up things won't get you into heaven, but it will help you remember that your relationship with God comes first.

When Jesus asks you to give up something you love for him, it might feel impossible. But he would say the same thing to you as he said about that rich man on the dusty road: "With man this is impossible, but not with God; all things are possible with God."

Is there anything standing in the way of your love for God? Is there anything more important to you than him? Can you talk to him about it?

Hurry Up—No, Wait

Desire without knowledge is not good—how much more will hasty feet miss the way!
PROVERBS 19:2

Have you ever wanted something so badly that you'd give just about anything to get it? Maybe it was a possession, a date, or a friendship. Sometimes our desires get the best of us, and we forget that what we want might not be worth the tradeoff.

One day, a guy in the Bible named Esau was so hungry he begged his brother, Jacob, to give him the food he'd just prepared. Esau didn't want to go through the trouble of making something for himself, and in his desire to get what he wanted, he promised his little brother something huge: that Jacob could have everything Esau would inherit from their very rich father.

Esau lost out that day by giving up what he treasured most. Next time you really, really want something, stop and count the cost. Are you willing to take something you want even if it doesn't belong to you? Are you willing to stop being yourself so your crush or your friend will like you? In the end, will it be worth it? Making fast decisions is a quick way to fall into sin. Don't act in a hurry. Give it some time and think it through.

Dear God, keep me from making hasty decisions. Help me think through what's right and what honors you. In Jesus' name, amen.

He Really is Coming Back

Let us hold unswervingly to the hope we profess, for he who promised is faithful.

HEBREWS 10:23

God promised Abraham a son. In fact, God promised him there would one day be as many people in his family as there were stars in the sky. But as Abraham approached 80, 90, and 100 years old—he started to think it might not happen. In spite of Abraham's doubts, God gave him a son when he was 100 years old. As a result, Abraham's grandchildren, great-grandchildren, and other descendants do outnumber the stars.

Sometimes it might feel like God's promise to return to earth and bring us home to heaven will never happen. We might lose hope and forget that he isn't looking at the same calendar we are. We might get sucked into everyday life: school, sports, homework, or family. Don't get so caught up that you forget that God will keep his promise. Jesus is coming—his word is true. Will you keep believing him?

Dear God, help me to believe you when you say you're returning to take me home to heaven with everyone who loves you. Help me live every day putting you first and thinking about your return. I know you're always working, even when I can't see. In Jesus' name, amen.

DAY 196

The Great Scavenger Hunt

By faith Abraham, when called to go to a place he would later receive as his inheritance, obeyed and went, even though he did not know where he was going.

HEBREWS 11:8

Have you ever started a scavenger hunt not knowing where you'll end up? Each stop gives you a clue to the next place you'll head until finally every clue is gathered and you reach your destination.

God asked Abraham to pack up his family and take them somewhere—but Abraham wasn't sure where. He had to have faith to head out on an adventure that he didn't know anything about.

It's possible God's going to take *you* on an adventure that's unfamiliar. It might be to a new home or a new school. It will feel hard at first to trust him because you're not sure how any of this is going to end up—but like Abraham, you can trust that God's taking care of you even when life feels uncertain. You don't have to be afraid—he'll never leave you on your own. He's with you on this great adventure.

Dear God, help me to trust you when life changes. Help me to know you're in control and you're directing every step I take. In Jesus' name, amen.

They're Cheering for You

Therefore, since we are surrounded by such a great cloud of witnesses, let us throw off everything that hinders and the sin that so easily entangles. And let us run with perseverance the race marked out for us,

HEBREWS 12:1

When you go to a basketball game, all eyes are on the court. If the score is close, fans yell and cheer and remind the players that they can win. If you're on the court, you might feel a rush of energy every time the crowd shouts your name.

The author of Hebrews said he had friends cheering him on when things got tough. He wasn't talking about the friends he saw in everyday life—he was talking about people who were already in heaven. Did you know there's a crowd of people cheering you on too? If you have loved ones in heaven, they're proud of you. If you don't have loved ones in heaven, there are still Christians who believe in you. The writer called them a cloud of witnesses that surrounds you. On days when things are tough and it's hard to stand up for your faith, you can know there's a huge crowd cheering you on and that with God by your side, you'll finish your game strong.

Dear God, thank you for the others who have gone before me and know what I'm going through. Thank you for cheering for me too. Help me to stand firm when others challenge my faith. In Jesus' name, amen.

Second Chances

Because of the Lord's great love we are not consumed, for his compassions never fail. They are new every morning; great is your faithfulness.

LAMENTATIONS 3:22-23

Have you ever played a board game and realized you were losing badly? You might have felt a little discouraged because you knew you just couldn't come back from your loss. Then you remembered—when the game ended, you'd have a chance to start all over.

God's people needed a new start in a more serious way. Their wickedness was so great that they were sacrificing babies to other gods. Then someone named Josiah became king, and when he read the Word of God he realized how badly they'd hurt God. The entire nation repented and God saved them.

You'll never sin so badly that God won't forgive you. His mercy is endless—he wants so much for you to know his words and keep his commands. If you're feeling like he can't forgive you, he wants you to know that his mercy is new every morning. Confess your sin and he'll give you the chance to start all over again.

Dear God, I know that sometimes I fail you. Sometimes it feels like I just can't get it right. I pray that you'll forgive me and help me to live in obedience. Thank you for giving me a brand-new start. Amen.

DAY 199

Fed By Ravens

I am the only one left, and now they are trying to kill me too.
I Kings 19:10b

Sometimes it isn't popular to believe in God. It isn't popular to pray in the cafeteria or invite other people to church. It isn't popular to listen to your teachers or hang out with the shy kids. It can feel like a lot of pressure to always do the right thing, and sometimes you get tired.

Elijah was just about the most unpopular person of his time. When the wicked queen hunted and killed thousands of other prophets, Elijah was tired of standing up for God. He was so worn down that he fell asleep hiding in a cave. But God saw him, sent ravens to bring him food, and told Elijah to rest so he could regain his strength.

It's okay to feel tired sometimes. You're human, and doing the right thing can be hard. God understands when you need to get away and rest. When you're ready, if you ask him, he'll give you the strength you need to get back out there and do the right thing again.

Dear God, thank you for giving me strength to sometimes do hard things. Thank you for understanding that I'm human, and for giving me everything I need to love you and others. In Jesus' name, amen.

Little Seeds Grow

A man reaps what he sows.
GALATIANS 6:7B

Have you ever picked produce at a farm? Maybe you picked strawberries, blueberries, or watermelons. Did you watch the farmer plant those seeds? Did he do it that morning, water it, and then have the plant ready for you to pick by that afternoon? Of course not! Farmers plant seeds long before you see the results.

You might be doing good things for God, but you may not see the results right away. You may have told a friend about Jesus, but that friend didn't follow Jesus right away. Maybe you obeyed your parents, but they didn't seem to notice. Or maybe you studied for your test, but your grade still wasn't great.

God promises that when you plant good seeds—good actions—you'll eventually reap good things. You might not see the results of doing the right thing right away, but God sees and he keeps his promises.

Dear God, thank you for noticing when I plant good seeds. Thank you even when I have to wait a while—you promise that I'll reap good things from those good seeds. Help me to be patient and keep doing the right thing. Amen.

What's a Cupbearer?

I was cupbearer to the king.

NEHEMIAH 1:11B

The word "cupbearer" sounds a little strange—but that's exactly what Nehemiah was. His job was to bear or carry the king's cup to him. He didn't just carry the king's food and drinks—he tasted them first. It might sound a little rude to taste someone else's food, but that was part of  Nehemiah's job. If anyone had secretly poisoned it, the king would know not to eat or drink it if Nehemiah got sick or even died from the poison first.

Jesus is a lot like our cupbearer. He bore the consequences for our sin. Instead of him allowing us to suffer separation from God for what we've done, he chose to take the poisoned cup for us. When he died on the cross and conquered death, he took our punishment. Can you thank him for being your cupbearer today?

Dear Jesus, thank you for being my cupbearer. Thank you for taking the poison of my sin so that I can live forever. Help me always remember to be grateful for your sacrifice. Amen.

A Table with the Enemy

You prepare a Table before me in The presence of my enemies.
PSALM 23:5A

Being a leader isn't easy. King David even had to hide in caves from jealous people who tried to kill him. But in the middle of hiding, he wrote these words in a song to God: "You prepare a table before me in the presence of my enemies." God wasn't literally setting a table for David while his enemies watched, but he was with him and providing for him in the middle of his problems.

No matter how bad things get in your life, God is always going to take care of you. He's going to help you find food, clothing, and shelter. He's right in the middle of whatever's going on in your life, and no matter what he'll never leave you.

God has a special calling on your life, and that means things won't always be easy for you. Stick with him and he'll help you feel secure, even in the presence of your enemies.

Dear God, thank you for your protection. Thank you for keeping your hand on my life. I know I can lead like David. Help me trust you even when I feel surrounded by difficult circumstances. In Jesus' name, amen.

Never Too Late

Jesus answered him, "Truly I tell you, today you will be with me in paradise."

LUKE 23:43

While Jesus was dying, people said mean things to him—even the two thieves who were dying on the crosses next to him found the energy to make fun of him. At the last minute, though, one of the thieves cried out to Jesus, asking him to save him. Jesus said right away, "Today you will be with me in paradise." What a huge difference between two thieves—one man who never repented and one who at the very last moment realized Jesus was the only one who *could* save him.

Which man are you more like? Maybe like the first man on the cross, you've never called out to Jesus to save you. Or maybe you have and you know that one day you'll be with Jesus in paradise. No matter what, it's never too late. He wants to save you because he loves you.

Dear Jesus, help me to be like the man who called out to you. I want you to save me and take me home with you someday. In Jesus' name, amen.

Pour Out Your Heart

TrusT in him aT all Times, you people; pour ouT your hearTs To him,
for God is our refuge.

PSALM 62:8

What's the most disappointing thing that's ever happened to you? Were you cut from the soccer team? Did you fail your audition? Did you flunk your math test? Where did you go when that feeling of disappointment felt overwhelming?

God says you can pour out your heart to him when life is disappointing. That means you can tell him everything you're feeling. He can handle it no matter what you have to say, and he promises to be a refuge or a place of safety.

Don't let disappointment keep you from connecting with God. He's the only one who can really listen and understand.

Dear God, help me not to live in my disappointment. Thank you for being my refuge—a place where I can feel safe. I pour out my heart to you. I love you. Amen.

Welcome To the Family

'But we had to celebrate and be glad, because this brother of yours was dead and is alive again; he was lost and is found.'

Luke 15:32

In World War II, many people who stood up for the Jews were captured and sent away to prison camps. When the war was over, one of those prisoners, a woman named Corrie Ten Boom, traveled the world to tell about how God helped her in prison. At the end of one of her speeches, a man walked up to her. Her heart sank when she realized he was one of the cruelest prison guards. The man explained that he'd become a Christian, and asked if she could forgive him for what he'd done to her. For a moment she hesitated, then reached out and took his hand in hers.

It might be hard to be accepting when one of your enemies comes to know Jesus. It might not seem fair when that person has hurt you so much. But God says he shows mercy to people who are kind and people who are not. We don't get to decide whether someone else gets to enter God's family. But you can choose your attitude when they do. Will you, like Corrie Ten Boom, rejoice when your enemy is saved?

Dear God, help me to be happy when my enemies come to know you. Help me to be an example to them so that they will want to know you. In Jesus' name, amen.

Taking the Blame

As a sheep before its shearers is silent, so he did not open his mouth.
ISAIAH 53:7B

What if someone accused you of stealing at school but you didn't do it? What if you knew who did, were called into the principal's office, and she wanted to know the whole story? Would you stand up for yourself, or would you take the blame? It wouldn't make any sense to take the fall for something someone else did.

When Jesus was brought before a judge for some things he didn't do, he could have defended himself. He was God's perfect son—he'd hadn't done anything wrong. Instead, he chose to be "like a sheep before its shearers" and not make a sound. When he was questioned, he didn't even open his mouth. That's how great his love is for you; he willingly took the blame so he could die on the cross for your sin. The Bible says there's no greater love than willingly laying down your life for a friend. Can you thank Jesus for loving you enough to take your sin?

Dear Jesus, thank you for loving me so much that you took the blame of my sin away from me. Please show me how to love others in the same way you love me. Amen.

H-A-P-P-Y

And even though you do not see him now, you believe in him and are filled with an inexpressible and glorious joy.

1 PETER 1:8b

Can you fill in the blank? Happiness is when _____. You might've said happiness is when your homework's done, or happiness is when summer break comes, or when your mom cooks your favorite meal. It's true that all those things can give you a good feeling, but that feeling doesn't last forever.

There is a joy that comes from God that nothing can take away. It's a happiness you have even when you're staring at a mountain of homework, you're in the middle of the school year, or your mom makes spinach casserole for dinner. No matter what happens during your day, you can have true happiness in the fact that God is your help. He's been there since before the world was made, and he'll be there when you meet him in heaven.

The Bible says your hope is in him—and that's one thing you can know won't change. Will you ask him to help you find your happiness in him today?

Dear God, thank you because my happiness in you doesn't have to change. You're the same no matter how my day's going, and I'm thankful I can always count on you. In Jesus' name, amen.

I Have Eyes in My Heart?

I pray that the eyes of your heart may be enlightened.
EPHESIANS 1:18A

Have you ever seen a picture with another picture hidden inside? You might've had to stare at it for a long time and turn your head a certain way, but suddenly you see what had been there all along.

Before you trusted Jesus as your savior, you might have not seen the truths in the Bible. It was a lot like looking at that optical illusion, and you couldn't see what was really there. You may have wondered what all this business in the Bible was about … like putting others first, believing in things you couldn't see, and trusting a God who sometimes allows tough things in your life. Now that you're a Christian, though, it's a lot like changing your angle and suddenly seeing the real picture. The more you study the Bible, the more it makes sense.

Don't worry if you don't understand everything just yet. No one does. Do you know someone who can help you read through this book and work on it even more? If not, ask a Christian friend and they'll help you. You should enjoy your new 20/20 vision!

Dear God, thank you for helping me begin to understand your Word. Thank you for being with me and teaching me as I go. Help me to find others who can help me understand your Word. Amen.

Taking It Back

So all the officials and people who entered into this covenant agreed that they would free their male and female slaves and no longer hold them in bondage. They agreed, and set them free. But afterward they changed their minds and took back the slaves they had freed and enslaved them again.

JEREMIAH 34:10–11

Have you ever felt guilty for a sin in your life? God's Word was helping you see right from wrong, and maybe you promised him you wouldn't do that wrong thing anymore. Then some time passed and you found yourself falling back into your old habit. Your sin didn't seem so wrong anymore—you broke your promise to God.

When God's people told him they didn't want to keep slaves anymore, they set them free. Then they changed their minds—they took their slaves back. How very sad God must have been for those people who were hurt. When we break our promises to God, it breaks his heart. He knows we can do what's right, but we've chosen our own way anyway. Have you made a promise to God that you've forgotten or broken? How can you make it right? He's waiting to forgive and help you do the right thing.

Dear God, please help me keep my promises to you. Thank you for giving me the strength to do the right thing. Help me remember even after the feeling of guilt goes away that I need to do the right thing. In Jesus' name, amen.

Wisdom, Stature, and Favor

And Jesus grew in wisdom and stature, and in favor with God and man.
LUKE 2:52

Every time you go to the doctor she probably checks your height and your weight. Sometimes your size will be the same as your last visit, and sometimes you'll have had a growth spurt. It's not always important to grow after each visit, but it is important to gradually go from being a baby to an adult.

There are more ways to grow than just one. Even Jesus grew in more ways than just height and weight—he grew in wisdom and in favor with God and others. You're still learning how to love and obey God, and that takes a while. You're also still learning how to love and obey your parents and teachers. You don't grow all in one big leap. When you mess up, try again. Don't be too hard on yourself. As long as you're learning from your mistakes, you're growing.

Dear God, help me keep growing in my love for you and others. Thank you for understanding me because you were a kid once too. Help me follow your example and be more like you. Amen.

Making Excuses

"But I did obey the Lord," Saul said. "I went on the mission the Lord assigned me. I completely destroyed the Amalekites and brought back Agag their king. The soldiers took sheep and cattle from the plunder, the best of what was devoted to God, in order to sacrifice them to the Lord your God at Gilgal."

1 Samuel 15:20–21

Have your parents ever told you not to do something but you decided to do it anyway? Maybe you weren't supposed to stop by your friend's house after school or you weren't supposed to hang out with that one person who is a bad influence on you.

God told Saul and the Israelites to find and conquer their enemies, but not to bring back anything. King Saul didn't listen—he had the soldiers carry back the best animals they could find. When Samuel asked Saul why he'd disobeyed God, Saul told him that the soldiers had done it because they wanted to sacrifice the animals to God. He blamed someone else and made excuses.

When we do something wrong, we shouldn't make it look like someone else's fault or make excuses for doing what we've done. Instead, we can choose to own up to our mistakes and try to do the right thing next time.

Dear God, help me not to make excuses when I mess up. Help me to be honest about the choices I make, and to try hard to do the right thing next time. In Jesus' name, amen.

Find Your Creative Side

I praise you because I am fearfully and wonderfully made; your works are wonderful, I know that full well.

PSALM 139:14

Have you ever been on a hike and noticed a beautiful mountain ridge? Or stood on the beach and watched the blue-gray waves crash onto the shore? Maybe you've looked out the car window and noticed the sky lit up in gray and pink and orange. God is an amazing creator, and you're made in his image—you're made to be creative too!

Maybe you're good at designing things on the computer or creating an amazing picture on canvas. Maybe you can entertain young kids for hours and hours with your storytelling abilities. Or maybe you want to feel creative, but you're not quite sure where to start.

The best way to find your creative talents is to try lots of different things. If you're not enjoying the first one after a while, move on to the next. Keep dabbling until you find your creative side. It's in there! God says you're fearfully and wonderfully made—and part of that is being creative just like him.

Is there an art form you've always wanted to try? What kind of supplies will you need? Maybe you can ask your parents to help you figure out what you'd enjoy creating.

Obedience = Protection

My God sent his angel, and he shut the mouths of the lions. They have not hurt me, because I was found innocent in his sight. Nor have I ever done any wrong before you, Your Majesty.
DANIEL 6:22

Do you ever feel afraid when you need do the right thing? Maybe you're afraid of being made fun of—or maybe you're afraid you'll lose friends. Daniel was a normal person with normal emotions. He probably felt afraid when he chose to pray to God after the king made a law that people couldn't worship anyone but him.

When Daniel chose to do the right thing, God protected him. After Daniel was thrown into a cave with wild, hungry lions, God sent an angel to close the mouths of those lions to keep them from devouring Daniel.

You can be afraid and brave at the same time. The same God who helped Daniel can help you to stand up for what's right. God will be with you and give you just the right amount of courage at the right time. He will protect you.

Dear Jesus, thank you for protecting me even when I'm afraid. I put my trust in you. Help me to live for you even when I'm scared. In Jesus' name, amen.

Being a Team

Do Two walk TogeTher unLesS They have agreed To do So?
AMOS 3:3

Have you ever been paired up with a project partner you didn't get along with? Maybe you didn't like each other, or maybe they didn't do their fair share of the work.

Someone wise once said, "There's no I in the word team." In other words, it's not about you. When you're working as a team, you should be thinking about the goal you all want to accomplish—not what *you* can get out of it. That means even if you don't like your project partner, or you're not getting along with your sibling, you can still find something to agree about.

Whether it's at school or home, if you're having trouble feeling like part of a team, look for something you all want to accomplish. Once you've agreed on that, you can all go in the same direction. You'll feel glad in the end that you overcame your differences and completed something amazing.

Dear God, help me learn how to work as part of a team. Help me see a common goal that will bring my teammates and me together. In Jesus' name, amen.

221

Special to God's Heart

The king asked, "Is there no one still alive from the house of Saul to whom I can show God's kindness?" Ziba answered the king, "There is still a son of Jonathan; he is lame in both feet."

2 SAMUEL 9:3

What are some ways you and your friends are different from each other? One of you might walk with your feet, and another might ride in a wheelchair. One of you might have lots of words, and another might have a different way of talking.

Whatever differences you or your friends have, God has a special place for those who feel a little different. He even reminded King David to reach out to a man who couldn't walk, and the king asked the man to eat at his table every day. God made you—and your friends—just the way you are for a reason. He loves you and calls you his children!

Dear God, thank you for making me just the way I am for a reason. Thank you for loving me.

God's Not Prejudiced

Then Peter began to speak: "I now realize how true it is that God does not show favoritism."

ACTS 10:34

In the New Testament church, it took a while for Jewish Christians to realize that people of other ethnicities were also able to be Christians. At first they thought that because Jesus was a Jew, the gospel was only for Jews. But things changed when they began to realize Christ didn't show favoritism to anyone because of their ethnicity. He died for the Jewish people and for people all over the world.

Have you ever heard someone say something unkind about someone's skin color, where they live, or where they go to school? God doesn't pick favorites, and it's not kind or fair for others to pick favorites, either. Next time you hear someone make a negative comment about another person, maybe you could say something to stand up for that person. You can make a difference by refusing to play favorites.

Dear God, help me not to be prejudiced. Help me to love everyone and remember that you came for not just me—you came for everyone. In Jesus' name, amen.

God Thinks You're Amazing

The crowds that went ahead of him and those that followed shouted, "Hosanna to the Son of David!" "Blessed is he who comes in the name of the Lord!" "Hosanna in the highest heaven!"
MATTHEW 21:9

One day Jesus rode through the streets of Jerusalem on a donkey. The people he had healed and taught shouted, "Hosanna in the highest heaven!" They were praising God, and welcoming Jesus—hoping he would be their earthly king. Just one week later, some of those same people sent him to die on a cross.

People's opinions can change very quickly—that's why Jesus didn't put his hope in what other people said about him. He was too busy obeying and loving his heavenly Father to care what others thought. In the same way, you don't need to be overly bothered about what other people say about you. One day your friends might be feeling nice, and another they might say things about you that aren't kind or even true. What matters most is what God thinks about you as his child: he loves you. He cares about you. And he knows that when he made you, he made something amazing.

Dear God, no matter how much other peoples' opinions change, yours stays the same. Thank you for thinking that when you made me, you made something amazing. I love you. Amen.

Faith to Believe

They found the stone rolled away from the tomb, but when they entered, they did not find the body of the Lord Jesus.

LUKE 24:2-3

When Jesus died, his friends went to his grave—it was a huge cave with the opening covered by a stone. When they got there, the stone protecting the entrance was rolled away and Jesus' body was missing. His friends began to cry—they thought someone had stolen his body. Suddenly an angel appeared and said, "Why do you seek the living among the dead?"

Jesus had come back to life just like he'd promised, but it was still hard for his followers to believe it. Sometimes it might be hard for you to have faith too. You might have trouble believing he's with you when you feel alone, or you might have trouble believing he answers your prayers. But Jesus promises that when you're feeling doubts about him, he can give you faith. After all, his body isn't in the grave—he's alive and powerful, ready to help you.

One way Jesus helps you is by putting other Christians in your life to help you sort through your doubts. Who can you talk to when things get tough?

When He Doesn't Rescue

And at three in the afternoon Jesus cried out in a loud voice, "Eloi, Eloi, Lema sabachthani?" (which means "My God, my God, why have you forsaken me?").

MARK 15:34

Have you ever asked God to stop your suffering? Maybe someone posted a horrible picture of you on social media, and even your friends made fun of you. Or you lost someone you loved. Maybe your parents didn't stay together, even when you asked God to make things okay again.

When Jesus was on the cross, he asked God why he had forsaken him. God had the power to change his plan and command Jesus to come down, but he didn't do it. He had a bigger plan in mind—he knew Jesus had to go through that horrible thing so that we could be saved.

Sometimes God rescues us from our problems, and sometimes he gives us courage to go through them. Next time you're worried because God hasn't saved you from your problems, remember that Jesus suffered too. God loves you and he'll give you strength to get through your problem.

Dear God, help me trust you even when I'm suffering. I know you have a bigger plan and you don't always choose to save me from my problems. Thank you for loving me and caring for me even in the middle of them. In Jesus' name, amen.

Slowing Down

BuT MarTha was disTracTed by aLL The preparaTions ThaT had To be made. She came To him and asked, "Lord, don'T you care ThaT my sisTer has LefT me To do The work by myseLf? TeLL her To heLp me!"
LUKE 10:40

Have you ever tried to do more than one thing at a time? What if you tried to listen to the radio, watch television, study for your test, and send a text message all at the same time? Sometimes you can multitask, but if you add too many things in it becomes impossible to focus.

When you have too many activities going at once, you can get distracted in your walk with God too. You might get so busy doing things for Jesus, that you forget to spend time with Jesus. Maybe you're doing a lot to help at church—all good things—but you feel far away from God. You could be singing in the choir and helping in the nursery and volunteering at youth group, or whatever activities you're doing. If you're participating in more than a few ways to serve, it might be a good idea to take a break and just listen in youth group every once in a while. It's great to serve Jesus, but don't forget he wants you to spend time with him too.

Dear Jesus, thank you for giving me ways to serve you. Help me to remember that you also want me to spend time with you. I love you. In Jesus' name, amen.

Everything You Need

> "Apart from me you can do nothing."
> **JOHN 15:5b**

What if you were playing basketball and your entire team left the court? It was just you against the other team—five against one. You'd have to play offense and defense. No matter how good you were at the game, it would be an impossible task. You wouldn't be able to do anything apart from your team.

God says you can't do anything apart from him, either. He's not only your teammate—he's your maker. He gave you breath in your lungs when you were born. He gave you a brain in your head that makes decisions and comes up with ideas. He gives you food and drink and everything it takes to stay alive.

Can you thank him for making you and giving you everything you need?

Dear Jesus, thank you for making me. Thank you for giving me abilities and gifts and food and drink. You're more than just a teammate. Apart from you I can do nothing. Amen.

Just a Shepherd Boy

But David said to Saul, "Your servant has been keeping his father's sheep. When a lion or a bear came and carried off a sheep from the flock, I went after it, struck it and rescued the sheep from its mouth. When it turned on me, I seized it by its hair, struck it and killed it."

I Samuel 17:34-35

David was just a boy when he fought the giant named Goliath. None of the adults in the army were brave enough to face the huge man, but God gave David courage to do what no one else would do—and he did it with just a sling and a stone.

When King Saul asked David how he would fight the giant when he was only a boy, David said he knew God would help him overcome Goliath because he'd helped him overcome giant problems in the past. As a shepherd, David had protected his sheep from a lion and a bear—but he knew it was God who helped him do it.

What are some giant problems God has helped you overcome? If you keep a list of those times when God helped you, you won't feel so scared when it's time to overcome your next problem.

Dear God, thank you for helping me overcome problems. Thank you for being the one who gives me the courage to do things even when I'm young. In Jesus' name, amen.

DAY 223

He Chose You

In your relationships with one another, have the same mindset as Christ Jesus.

PHILIPPIANS 2:5

Imagine you have the perfect house—it's everything you've ever dreamed of. Your room is just the right size, your bed is just the right comfort, and your pool is nice and cool. Your neighbors are pretty awesome too. Now imagine you decide to move. What would make you do that?

There's only one thing that made Jesus leave heaven, his truly perfect home with his father, to come to earth: you. He chose you over the most beautiful, peaceful place you could ever imagine. The Bible says you should have the same attitude toward others as he had toward you—sometimes you should choose what they need instead of what you want.

How can you choose someone else today? Can you let your sister pick what's for dinner? Can you let your classmate answer the question instead of you? Can you take a step back in the lunch line?

Dear God, help me to choose someone else today. Help me remember that you chose me—thank you for that. In Jesus' name, amen.

My Apologies

Therefore, if you are offering your gift at the altar and there remember that your brother or sister has something against you, leave your gift there in front of the altar. First go and be reconciled to them; then come and offer your gift.

MATTHEW 5:23–24

Have you ever said something you wished you could take back? Maybe you were talking with a friend and before you knew it, you were gossiping about another person. Maybe you were in an argument with your mom, and angry words came out of your mouth or you were jealous of your brother and you said something unkind because of it. You knew you needed to apologize, but where should you start?

It's important when you're apologizing to be sincere—the apology should come from your heart, or the other person will be able to tell you don't mean it. Maybe you weren't the only one who said or did angry things—maybe they did too. But even if you weren't the only one who did wrong, you shouldn't make excuses for what you did when you apologize. You should simply tell them 1) you know what you did that was wrong, and 2) why you're sorry you did that wrong thing.

We all do things that we need to apologize for. The most important part is that you make things right as soon as you can.

Dear Jesus, help me to make things right when I make someone sad. Thank you for always forgiving me too. I want to love others with my words. In your name, amen.

You Have a Free Will

I have chosen the way of faithfulness; I have set my heart on your laws.

PSALM 119:30

Sometimes you're going to want your own way. No matter what the Bible says, or how well it explains things, your heart is still going to want to do what you want to do. You can choose obedience or disobedience, but obedience is going to make your relationship with God stronger.

God could have made people like robots—he could have hardwired us with the ability to only obey. But how boring would that be? Instead, he made us in his image—with a free will to choose right or wrong.

Aren't you glad you aren't a robot? Will you choose to use your free will in a way that helps instead of hurts others? Next time you're tempted to go your own way, think about how it might affect your relationship with God and others. He loves you enough to create you with the ability to choose well.

Dear God, thank you for giving me a free will. Help me to follow you, even when my heart wants its own way. Thank you for loving me and wanting the best for me. In Jesus' name, amen.

Helping Hands

For even The Son of Man did not come To be served, but To serve, and To give his Life as a ransom for many.
MARK 10:45

When someone does something thoughtful for you, does it make you feel good? Maybe you forgot your silverware, and someone brought some to the lunch table for you. Or you dropped your books in the hall-way, and someone helped you pick them up. Or maybe you forgot to do your chores, so your mom did them for you instead. Those people were serving you.

There are lots of ways to serve other people, even at church. Have you noticed how your youth pastor has a lot to do? Maybe you could ask him if you can help get the room ready on Sunday mornings. Is your church nursery missing a volunteer? Ask if they need help with the little kids one morning. Or is there a big meal coming up? You could ask if you could help in the serving line. Keep your eyes open for opportunities to help others, because even Jesus came to serve. You might brighten someone's day just like it brightens yours when others serve you.

Dear God, help me look for ways to serve you at church. Thank you for setting an example for me by coming to serve. I love you. Amen.

Out of Luck

BUT blessed is The one who Trusts in The LORD, whose confidence is in him.

JEREMIAH 17:7

When something good happens to one of your friends, you might tell them, "You're so lucky!" "Luck" is a word you hear all the time: someone's lucky when they're chosen as class president, get an awesome birthday present, or get to go on a fun vacation. But we should be careful how we use the word "luck."

Nothing happens in our lives because of luck, because luck is something that's brought on by chance, not by God's help. The Bible makes it very clear that everything good we have, even things we work for, are gifts from God. He gives us the ability to work for good things. So instead of thinking you're lucky, thank God for what he's given or done for you.

Dear Jesus, I don't have to put my trust in luck—I have something much more reliable: you! Thank you for providing such good things for me. In your name, amen.

DAY 228

Meekness

Blessed are the meek, for they will inherit the earth.
MATTHEW 5:5

When you hear the word "meek," what do you think? It might rhyme with the word "weak," but it isn't the same thing at all. In this case, meekness means being gentle with others and willing to serve them. That doesn't mean you let people treat you badly, it just means you're choosing to put other people first sometimes. Jesus did that when he quietly washed his disciples' feet at the Last Supper. He was the God of the universe, but he got down on his hands and knees—something a household servant would usually do—and took on the dirtiest job in the house.

When you're walking through your day, what are some ways you can practice meekness? Could you clean the bathroom for your mom, carry a lunch tray for a friend, take the trash out for your brother? Jesus set the example for how to gently serve others, and when you follow it you're learning to be more and more like him.

Dear God, help me to learn meekness by gently serving others. Help me to follow your example so I can be more like you. I love you. In Jesus' name, amen.

Sharing Bitterness

See To iT That no one falls short of The grace of God and that no bitter root grows up To cause Trouble and defile many.
HEBREWS 12:15

Have you ever tasted bitter food? Some roots like ginger are sweet, and some roots like curcumin are very bitter. If you did taste a food that was bitter, would you share it with all your friends? They probably wouldn't like it much.

The Bible talks about another type of bitterness that's not good for our friends—the kind of bitter feelings that happen when someone hurts you. Hebrews 12:15 says when you don't forgive someone, that feeling can take root in your heart like a strong, bitter root. When you stay angry for a while, it grows and grows. Pretty soon everyone around you can tell that you're feeling bitter toward the person who hurt you, and they might start having hard feelings toward that person for what they did too.

Is there a root of bitterness in your heart toward someone? Instead of talking badly to your friends about someone, can you talk to God about it? He can help you forgive the person who hurt you so that more people won't be hurt.

Dear God, please help me forgive the person who hurt me. Help me not to talk badly about them to other people. Help me to forgive them with the same power that helped you forgive me. In Jesus' name, amen.

Feeling Down?

Why, my soul, are you downcast? Why so disturbed within me? Put your hope in God, for I will yet praise him, my Savior and my God.
PSALM 43:5

Have you ever felt really down? You might've had a bad day at school, or even a bad week. Something might've caused your sadness, or maybe it just seemed to come out of nowhere. How did you try to cheer yourself up?

The Psalms show us that it's okay to feel sad, and it's okay to talk to God about it. Many different people wrote this book of the Bible—but most of the Psalms have this in common: they're written when someone is feeling at least a little bit down. The best thing about the Psalms is that they usually end on a happy note. After all the sadness and questions, the writers usually finish by thanking God that he's in control.

When you talk to God about your sadness, tell him exactly how you feel. He's there to listen and he cares about you. But when you're done telling him about your sadness, thank him that he's taking care of you. Put your trust in him and know that he won't let you feel sad forever.

If you have a feeling of sadness that sticks around for more than a day or two, you should talk to an adult you trust about it. They can listen to what's going on in your life. They can also help you find ways to feel better.

A Cup of Cold Water

And if anyone gives even a cup of cold water to one of these little ones who is my disciple, truly I tell you, that person will certainly not lose their reward.

MATTHEW 10:42

Did you know there are millions of people around the world who don't have clean water? They can't walk up to the sink or refrigerator and fill their cups. They might not even be able to walk to a well or a river to get what they need.

There are things you can do to help people who don't have food or water. You're not too young to do something that can make a big difference. If you're not sure where to start, ask your parents or youth pastor to help you find a missionary who helps people who are hungry or thirsty. You may not be able to travel yet, but you can do extra chores to raise money for someone to dig a well or plant a garden. Some missions will even let you write to people when you send money to help them.

Jesus says when you help others who have less than you, giving just one drink of cold water makes a difference. What can you do today?

Dear God, help me remember people who need food and water. Help me to not just remember them, but to do something for them. Thank you for providing everything I need. In Jesus' name, amen.

A Great Reward

Their work will be shown for what it is, because the Day will bring it to light. It will be revealed with fire, and the fire will test the quality of each person's work. If what has been built survives, the builder will receive a reward.

I Corinthians 3:13-14

Sometimes it might seem like no one notices when you do the right thing. It might seem like everyone's so busy they forget to tell you, "Good job!" It might seem like there's no reward for being obedient to your parents or to God.

Did you know that God notices your good works, and he's proud of you? He promises that when you do the right thing, he'll reward you. You'll see some of his rewards on earth, but he's especially saving rewards for you in heaven. When you have a good attitude, when you tell someone else about him, when you love other people, he notices all of that.

When you get to heaven, God has a special reward prepared for you. You can't see it now, but it's coming. Keep doing the right thing, and know that when no one else seems to notice, God does.

Dear God, thank you for noticing when I'm trying hard to please you. Thank you for not forgetting the good things I'm doing. In Jesus' name, amen.

Your Favorite Song

About midnight Paul and Silas were praying and singing hymns to God, and the other prisoners were listening to them.

ACTS 16:25

Have you ever been feeling a little down and decided to turn on the radio? If you turned it to an upbeat station, did your feet start to tap a little and your voice start to hum? Did you notice how, after a while, your whole attitude started to change? God created music as a powerful gift that can calm us and help us feel better. Most of all, God created music as a way to worship him.

When Paul and Silas were imprisoned for their faith, they used the gift of music to help them focus on God. Instead of choosing to despair, they

chose to sing songs of praise. Their music probably brought comfort to the other prisoners and helped the men feel better.

Be careful what kinds of music you listen to. The words can cause you to feel down, or they can cause you to give thanks to God. What are some good examples of songs that help change your heart for the better?

Dear God, thank you for making the powerful gift of music. Help me put good kinds of music in my mind—music that will help me worship you and feel good too. I love you. Amen.

In the Battle

For our struggle is not against flesh and blood, but against the rulers, against the authorities, against the powers of this dark world and against the spiritual forces of evil in the heavenly realms.

EPHESIANS 6:12

In almost any book you read, or any movie you watch, there's a villain and a hero. The villain's job is to ruin the good work the hero is trying to do. The same is true in your every-day life: there's an invisible battle happening—good vs. evil—God vs. Satan.

Satan already knows that God's going to win the battle, but he's trying to win as many people to his side as he can until Jesus comes back. There are some people who don't realize they're being used by Satan to help him with that goal—they say and do unkind things, and Satan uses those unkind things to hurt or discourage God's people.

Next time someone says or does something unkind to you, try to look past what that person's done and remember that your battle isn't against that person. Your battle is against Satan, God's enemy. One day God will silence that enemy and you'll never feel hurt or discouraged again. Until then, remember whose side you're on. God loves you and he'll take care of you. He'll help you love those who have hurt you instead of hurting those people back.

Dear God, thank you for protecting me in this battle until you come again. Thank you for not asking me to do this alone. In Jesus' name, amen.

On Screen

Finally, brothers and sisters, whatever is true, whatever is noble, whatever is right, whatever is pure, whatever is lovely, whatever is admirable—if anything is excellent or praiseworthy—think about such things.

PHILIPPIANS 4:8

Do you have a favorite television show? What are the characters like? Where do they live? What do they do? How do they talk?

Did you know that the things you hear and see stay with you long after you turn off your TV? Weeks, months, and even years later you can still quote your favorite movie. That's why it's important to pick shows and movies that are going to help you want to be a better person.

When you watch shows that have violence or bad language, those actions and words tempt you to do and say things you shouldn't. In the same way, when you watch shows with characters who say and do good things, you may find yourself wanting to say and do good things.

Make a list of your favorite TV shows. Are there any you should add to that list? Are there any you should take away?

Dear God, help me put good things in front of my eyes. Help me to honor you and love others better because of what I'm watching. In Jesus' name, amen.

Lord of All

And every Tongue acknowledge That Jesus Christ is Lord,
To The glory of God The Father.

PHILIPPIANS 2:11

Sometimes things are going to go exactly like you want them to. You'll get good grades at school. You'll play well and your team will win. You'll listen for your parents to start arguing and it won't happen. Life will seem like everything's under control.

Then there will be other times you struggle with your grades even when you study hard. Your team might not win even when you play your best. And your parents might start arguing again even when they'd stopped for a while. The feeling you had that everything was under control can go away quickly.

Did you know that Jesus is Lord of the good and bad times in your life? Lord means master. Even when things don't feel like they're going okay, he still has everything under control. You don't have to worry about controlling everything—you can trust him and know that he'll take care of you no matter what.

Dear Jesus, thank you for being the Lord of my life. Thank you for taking care of me in the good times and the bad times. Thank you for helping me do my best while you take care of the results. Amen.

DAY 237

His Name Is Special

You shall not misuse the name of the LORD your God
EXODUS 20:7A

You hear it a lot on television and maybe even at school—people taking God's name in vain. To not say his name in a flippant way is one of the Ten Commandments. That's because God—the creator of the universe—deserves our respect.

How would you feel if every time something bad happened, someone said your name like a cuss word? Would that make you sad? That might be how God feels when we don't use his name with respect.

If you've made a habit of using God's name in vain, it's never too late to stop. Ask him for help, and ask one of your Christian friends to ask you from time to time how your language has been. It will take some practice to clean up your language, but it's worth the effort. God loves you and deserves your respect.

Dear God, help me respect you by not taking your name in vain. Thank you for being worthy of that respect. In Jesus' name, amen.

No Hate Here

Anyone who claims to be in the light but hates a brother or sister is still in the darkness.

1 John 2:9

"Hate" is a word people say a lot. You might say you hate doing homework, brussels sprouts, or math homework. Usually that means you just don't like something, but what about when you feel real hate toward a person? Maybe someone hurt you, and it's not just that you don't like them—it's that you really think you hate them.

Hatred can be a big feeling. When you hate someone, you might also feel angry. You might think about ways you'd like to see them get hurt. You might even wish bad things for them. Eventually, that hatred can make you feel worried and sick.

It's not good for your body or your heart when you hold on to hatred. God wants to help you let it go so you can move onto better feelings and love your enemies. Will you ask him to help you do that today?

Dear Jesus, when I feel hate toward someone, would you help me forgive them? Help me remember that you give me the power to forgive instead of hate. In your name, amen.

Thanks A Lot

And be Thankful.
COLOSSIANS 3:15B

What if you did something nice for someone and they didn't say thank you? Would that make you want to do something nice for them again or would you feel discouraged?

When someone does something nice for you, it's important to remember to say thank you. When your dad does your laundry or your mom brings home dinner, it makes them happy when you thank them. When your sister helps you with your homework or your brother lets you use the bathroom first, it makes them happy to hear that you noticed. There are a lot of people you can thank every day—teachers, bus drivers, your friends, coaches, and family, just to name a few.

Is there anyone you need to thank today? You can say it with your words or write it in a note. You might just make someone's day by noticing their kindness!

Make a list of people you can thank for how they treat you. Now circle a name on that list and write that person a thank-you note.

Have You Told Them?

And you will be my witnesses in Jerusalem, and in all Judea and
Samaria, and to the ends of the earth.

Acts 1:8b

Right before Jesus went back to heaven, he told his friends
to go into the whole world and tell others about him. You
might not be able to go very far yet, but there are people right
where you are that you can tell about Jesus.

You might know a lot about the Bible, or you might feel like
you're just getting started. but no matter how much you know,
there's someone else who doesn't know as much as you do. Do
you have a little brother or sister you can read your devotions to?
Or can you help with the little kids' class at church? You might even have
a friend at school who doesn't know about God at all, and is just waiting
for someone to tell them.

No matter where you are, you can always find someone who needs to
know Jesus.

Dear Jesus, help me look for chances to tell my friends and family about
you. I hope they can learn about you just like I am. In Jesus' name, amen.

Celebrating You

The Lᴏʀᴅ delights in those who fear him, who put their
hope in his unfailing love.

Psalm 147:11

When you hear the word "celebration," what do you think of? Your birthday? Christmas? Other holidays?

Did you know that you're God's celebration? The Bible says he delights in you. When he looks at you, his eyes light up. You're his special child. Maybe you make his feet tap a little bit. Maybe he sings a happy song when he watches you or cheers for you when you're playing in that big game. Did you know he even loves to watch over you when you sleep?

No matter what you do, good choices or bad choices, God celebrates you—your life, your uniqueness, everything about you. When he made you, he knew he made something good. So next time someone tries to tell you you're not amazing, you can just smile and disagree—because God, your Father, says you're worth celebrating.

Dear God, thank you for celebrating me. Thank you for celebrating me enough that you want to spend forever with me some day. I love you. Amen.

A Sarcastic Answer

Instead, speaking the truth in love, we will grow to become in every respect the mature body of him who is the head, that is, Christ.

EPHESIANS 4:15

Have you ever said something sarcastically? Maybe you told your mom, "I'm so excited to go to the store with you," but you rolled your eyes when you said it. Or you told your friend you liked his shoes, but you said it in a mocking voice. Saying things in a sarcastic way can hurt other people's feelings. God gave you your voice so you could love others not tear them down.

Next time you feel like using sarcasm, think about how it would make you feel if someone spoke that way to you. Then use your words to respectfully say what you really mean. You can build someone up instead of bringing them down with what you say. You'll find it makes you and others much happier.

Dear God, help me to remember to use my words to love others. Help me remember how the same actions and words would make me feel if someone acted that way toward me. In Jesus' name, amen.

DAY 243

Giving Back

Honor The Lord with your wealth, with The firstfruits of all your crops.

PROVERBS 3:9

What's one way you can show God that you're thankful for everything he's given you? By giving some of it back to him! In the Old Testament, God wanted his people to offer ten percent of everything back to him—animals, fruits, vegetables, and money. You're not going to empty your dinner plate into the offering plate at church, but you can give back some of the money you've earned to say thank you to Jesus. If you earn ten dollars, you can give one dollar back to God—that's ten percent. If you earn one hundred dollars, you can give back ten dollars. The amount doesn't have to be exactly ten percent, but every bit you give back to him will show that you're grateful for everything he's given you.

Dear God, thank you for all you've given me. Help me show my gratitude by giving some back to you. In Jesus' name, amen.

How Would You Feel?

Let Love and faithfulness never leave you; bind Them round your neck, write Them on The tablet of your heart.

PROVERBS 3:3

Have you ever teased your brother about the girl he likes at school? Or teased your best friend about tripping over her shoelaces? What about your mom—have you ever teased her about a bad haircut?

Some teasing can be good-natured, but you can always tell when it's gone too far if the other person looks hurt or angry. Think about something your friends tease you about: maybe you're kind of clumsy and always bumping into things—you might think it's funny and laugh along, or it might make you feel self-conscious and upset. Or maybe you can't carry a tune, so you sing off-key just to be funny. If you're embarrassed, though, you might not think playful teasing is fun at all. Your friends all have things they're self-conscious about, and you should apologize if your teasing goes too far. Even if you didn't mean to hurt someone else's feelings, make sure to say you're sorry. It's better to be careful than to risk losing a friend.

Is there someone you've teased that took it the wrong way? Have you had a chance to tell them you're sorry? If not, be sure to do that the next time you see them.

DAY 245

Fully Committed

And may your hearts be fully committed To The LORD our God, To
Live by his decrees and obey his commands, as at This Time.

I KINGS 8:61

When you go to a wedding, the bride and groom stand up and promise to love each other. They're promising to be devoted—to stick with each other even when things get tough. But married people aren't the only ones who can practice devotion.

You can practice devotion to God when things get tough and do not make sense. When someone makes fun of your faith in God, you can be devoted to him even when others aren't kind. When God asks you to do something hard, you can be devoted to him by obeying even when you don't feel like it. When you're devoted to God, you'll know that your relationship with him is getting stronger.

Dear God, help me to be devoted to you even when it's hard. Help me to stick with you in the good times and the bad. Thank you for being devoted to me too. In Jesus' name, amen.

DAY 246

Truth Doesn't Change

I The Lord do not change.
MALACHI 3:6A

There are some things we know are true: we know the sky is blue, the grass is green, and the sun rises in the east and sets in the west. These are things we call "absolute truths."

Some people don't believe in absolute truths. They say things like, "What's your truth is your truth, and what's my truth is my truth." They don't want to believe that some things are right and some are wrong. For example, God says that hitting your sister, gossiping about your friends, and cheating on a test are all wrong. He gives us other truths in the Bible, too—things that are absolutely true all of the time.

No matter what others try to say, God's Word is absolutely true all the time. He doesn't change, and that's the absolute truth!

Dear God, thank you for giving me absolute truth so I can know how to obey you. Thank you that I can count on your Word to help me to make good choices. In Jesus' name, amen.

Watering Weeds

We Take captive every Thought To make iT obedienT To ChrisT.
2 CORINTHIANS 10:5B

Have you ever noticed a weed in a flower garden? It starts out small, but if no one pulls it, it grows and grows until it's bigger than the other plants. Soon that ugly weed starts stealing rain and sunlight from the flowers.

Bad thoughts are like bad weeds in your mind. When a bad thought pops into your mind, it's not your fault. But you can choose to let it stay there or you can tell God you don't want that thought. If you have a mean thought about your mom, about hitting your sister, or if you have a bad thought about cheating on a test, you can choose not to give into those temptations.

Instead of watering the weeds that come into your head, pull them up roots and all by praying about them. God hears your prayers and will help you choose to do the right thing instead.

Dear God, help me to be careful about letting bad thoughts lead to bad actions. I know bad thoughts will sometimes come, but I don't have to live them out. Thank you for giving me the choice to do what's right! In Jesus' name, amen.

Who's Your Mentor?

Whatever you have learned or received or heard from me, or seen in me—put it into practice.

PHILIPPIANS 4:9A

The apostle Paul told his young friend Timothy that Timothy could learn about God from him. Paul knew Timothy didn't have a dad who could teach him about God. He needed someone in his life to show him the right way to live.

God has people in your life who can teach you the right way to live. Those people are called *mentors*. Your mentor might be your mom, dad, or someone at church. If you're not sure if you have a mentor, think of someone you can ask for help. That person will probably be older than you and know more about the Bible than you. It should be someone you can tell your problems to and ask for help when you're having a hard time understanding something about God. God has a mentor for you—who do you think it could be?

Do you have a mentor in your life? If not, think about whom you could ask. That person can meet with you to talk about life and the Bible.

What's a Boundary?

Stay away from a fool, for you will not find knowledge on their lips.
PROVERBS 14:7

Is there a person in your life who won't leave you alone? Maybe they say mean things about what you're wearing, or they take the ball from you at recess. You might not feel like saying anything to that person because you're afraid of them, or you don't want to say anything because you don't want to hurt their feelings.

Did you know it's okay to set boundaries with someone who isn't respecting you? Setting boundaries means putting some space between you and that person. If they won't stop bullying you, it's okay to tell them to quit. If they don't stop, you should talk to an adult about separating that person from you so they can't keep hurting you. That might mean sitting at a different lunch table or taking a different bus. You are God's special creation, and it's not okay for anyone to bully his creation.

Dear God, help me stand up for myself when someone bullies me. Help me to find the help I need to get some space from any person who disrespects me. In Jesus' name, amen.

Falling from Heaven

I saw Satan fall like lightning from heaven.
LUKE 10:18B

Satan was one of God's most beautiful angels, but he wasn't happy to be an angel—he wanted to be God. He wanted to make the decisions, to rule the kingdom, and to have all the power. Because of Satan's pride, God had to make Satan leave heaven. Ever since, he has been God's enemy.

Satan is our enemy too. As children of God, Satan wants to trick us into thinking we can make all the decisions and have all the power we want. That was the same lie he told Adam and Eve—that they knew better than God did.

Any time you're tempted to believe that you know better than God, know that thought is just a lie Satan's always told God's children. We are created in God's image, but we aren't God. He still knows best, and he's still the king!

Dear God, thank you for helping me know I don't have to fall for Satan's tricks—I can be happy that you're God. I don't have to try to control everything. In Jesus' name, amen.

Your Family Needs You

BUT RUTH repLied, "Don't urge me to Leave you or to turn back from you. Where you go I wiLL go, and where you stay I wiLL stay.
RUTH 1:16A

When Ruth's husband died, she wanted to take care of her mother-in-law Naomi. So Ruth followed her on a long journey, back to her husband's homeland. At one point, her mother-in-law tried to get Ruth to turn around and go back home to her own country. But Ruth wanted to care for the woman she now saw as her mom.

You can be loyal to your family too. If bullies try to bother your brother or sister, you can stand up for them. If friends try to say your mom's being too strict, you can obey what she says anyway. And if your family's making a move and you don't feel like leaving all of your friends, you can choose not to complain. Your friends will change as you get older, but your family is forever.

Dear God, help me to be loyal to my family. Help me remember that they matter to me and to you. In Jesus' name, amen.

God's Gracious Hand

For the gracious hand of his God was on him. For Ezra had devoted
himself to the study and observance of the Law of the Lord, and
to teaching its decrees and laws in Israel.

EZRA 7:9b-10

The priest Ezra did amazing things for the Israelites. God
took him on a great adventure to help his people escape
the land of Babylon and return home to their own country.
The Bible says that God's gracious hand was on Ezra because
Ezra studied and taught God's Word to his people.

God's gracious hand is on your life when you follow his word
too. He promises that when you study and obey the Bible, he'll
bless you. As you grow, he can take you on a great adventure to
teach his Word to other people just like Ezra did. Can you be brave like
Ezra? Going on God's adventure takes courage—but with his hand on
your life, you can do anything God asks you to do.

Dear God, help me to be courageous like Ezra. Thank you for having
your hand on my life. In Jesus' name, amen.

It Can't Be Swept Away

When you pass Through The waters, I will be with you; and when
you pass Through The rivers, They will not sweep over you.

ISAIAH 43:2A

There will be times when it feels like you're living in a storm—not the
kind of storm that happens outside your window, but the kind of storm
that happens inside of you when life gets tough. You may feel sadness,
anger, and loss. It might seem like nothing will ever be the same again.
But no matter how bad things feel, God says the storms in your life can't
sweep his love away.

He loved you before you were born, and he will love you until the end
of your life and beyond. No matter what happens, his love is the one thing
that won't change. When you feel worried or upset, ask him to help you
remember how big his love is for you. No matter how big the storm is,
God's love is bigger still.

Dear God, thank you because your love can't be swept away. Thank
you because your love never changes. Thank you because I can always
depend on your love. In Jesus' name, amen.

Are You a Rebel?

The ways of The Lord are right; the righteous walk in them, but the rebellious stumble in them.

HOSEA 14:9B

What does it mean to be a rebel? To rebel means to go the opposite way. There's a good way to rebel, and a bad way to rebel. The good way to rebel is to walk the opposite way from sin. That means when your friends want you to do something that you know is against God's word, you can rebel against what they expect you to do and choose to do the right thing.

The not-so-good way to rebel is to go the opposite way from God's Word. That means you go outside instead cleaning your room. Or you make up excuses why you can't do your homework.

What kind of rebellion will you choose? Jesus wants to help you rebel against sin.

Dear God, help me to be a rebel against sin. Help me to choose you and your ways. Your way is right. In Jesus' name, amen.

Compassion for You

ReTurn To The Lord your God, for he is gracious and compassionate, slow To anger and abounding in Love, and he reLenTs from sending caLamiTy.

JOEL 2:13B

Some people see God as someone who sits and watches people, waiting to punish anyone who disobeys him. While it's true that God is holy and must punish sin, the Bible also says that he is gracious, compassionate, slow to anger, and abounding in love.

In the Old Testament when God's people kept disobeying him, he sent his prophets to warn them about his coming judgment. He did that because of his grace, compassion, and patience. God has grace, compassion, and patience for you too. When you make a wrong choice, he's not sitting in the sky hoping to punish you. He loves you and wants to help you make a better choice next time.

Dear God, help me to make good choices. Thank you for being gracious, compassionate, slow to anger, and abounding in love. In your name, amen.

Do You Have What It Takes?

He has shown you, O mortal, what is good. And what does the
Lord require of you? To act justly and to love mercy and to walk
humbly with your God.

MICAH 6:8

Have you ever wondered how much you need to do to please God? Would
it take going to church every Sunday, putting the most money in the
offering plate, going on a mission trip with your family, and feeding the
homeless every Wednesday?

In the Old Testament, God's people were having trouble deciding what
it would take to please God. They suggested offering all kinds of sacrifices to him, but God told them that pleasing him was more about what
was in their hearts than what was in their hands. He told them to act justly
(play fair), love mercy (be kind), and walk humbly with him (respect and
obey him). Those three things weren't just ways for them to please God.
They are ways for *you* to please him too. How can you play fair, show kindness, and obey God today?

Dear God, thank you for showing me what honors you. Help me to
please you by playing fair, showing kindness, and obeying you. In your
name, amen.

263

DAY 257

Choosing Sides

Whatever they plot against the LORD he will bring to an end.
NAHUM 1:9A

Do you like to be on the winning team? When you're playing soccer and your teammate scores a goal, do you let out a shout? When you're playing cards and your teammate wins a round, do you feel yourself smiling?

Did you know that choosing teams isn't just for games? You can choose teams in life too. You get to decide whether you're going to be on God's team or another team. When God was trying to get the people of Nineveh to stop sinning and follow him, he sent a warning: when they chose to do evil against him, God told them he would stop their plans. In the battle of good vs. evil, God is always going to win.

Have you told God that you want to be on his winning team? Even when others around you sometimes choose to do evil, you can choose to stand with God. It might not feel easy at first, but you can know that with God you'll always win in the end.

Dear God, help me to choose your team every day. Even when others do evil, you can help me do good. In Jesus' name, amen.

Are You Gentle?

Let your gentleness be evident to all.
PHILIPPIANS 4:5A

When you're upset, it's easy to speak in a voice that sounds mean. Maybe your mom asks you to do your chores but you're busy with something else, so you want to shout at her. Maybe your dad asks you to do your homework, but that makes you feel angry because you'd rather do something else.

Think about how you'd feel if someone shouted at you. Would it hurt your feelings? When you feel like responding in anger, take a deep breath first. Close your eyes and picture yourself being calm. Instead of shouting, practice using a gentle voice. Treat your parents how you'd like to be treated. Whenever possible, treat everyone in your life gently.

Dear God, help me treat my family and friends gently, especially when I feel angry. Show me how to be careful with them and what they're feeling. In Jesus' name, amen.

Finding Time

BUT seek first his kingdom and his righteousness, and all these things will be given to you as well.

MATTHEW 6:33

Do you ever feel like there's not enough time in your day to talk to God? How will you find time to read your Bible, pray, listen to worship music, and still get your homework done?

By being a little creative, you can find time for God. If you're having trouble remembering to stop and pray each day, tape a prayer list beside your bedroom door. You don't have to have your eyes closed—you can pick a prayer request and talk to God while you're walking up the hallway. What about reading your Bible? You can pack this devotional in your backpack and read it on the way to school or on the way home. And listening to Christian music? You can do that any time you're cleaning your room or riding in the car.

God likes to visit with you any time, and you'll find that if you get creative about it, you'll have plenty of time to spend with him.

Dear God, help me find time to visit with you. Thank you for giving me the chance to connect with you through your Word, prayer, and music. I love you. Amen.

What Love Looks Like

Love is patient, love is kind. It does not envy, it does not boast, it is not proud.

1 Corinthians 13:4

Think about someone who makes you feel loved. Who is it? Your mom? Your friend? Your teacher? What do they do that makes you feel loved?

When someone loves you well, you can go on to share that love with someone else. When you're patient, kind, not jealous, not bragging or proud—God says that's what love looks like. It means not complaining when your little sister asks you the same question one thousand times, treating someone else kindly when they do better than you on a test, or not bragging when you do the best on the next one. Sometimes loving others might feel like the opposite of what you want to do. But just remember how good you feel when someone else loves you. You can make a difference by loving someone else too.

Dear God, thank you for showing me what love is. Help me share your love with others. In Jesus' name, amen.

Your Good God

*The L*ORD *is good to all; he has compassion on all he has made.*
PSALM 145:9

Did you get to see the sunrise this morning? Did you notice the pink, yellow, and gray streaks across the sky? What about the last time it rained? Did you hear the pitter-patter of raindrops on the roof?

Your amazing, good God makes the world turn so that the sun rises every day. He sends rain so that plants can grow and you can have something to eat. He puts a roof over your head so that you can hear the sound of the rain every time it falls. Most importantly, he's so good that he sent Jesus to die for you.

Sometimes you might forget about his goodness. When tough stuff happens, God might feel far away. Next time you're feeling discouraged by your problems, take a step outdoors. Feel the wind blow across your face, or watch the sun set in the sky. Know that God is good, and he'll never let you down.

Dear God, thank you because you're always good. Thank you because your goodness makes the world turn, and provides for every need I have. In Jesus' name, amen.

A Firm Foundation

Therefore everyone who hears these words of mine and puts them into practice is like a wise man who built his house on the rock. The rain came down, the streams rose, and the winds blew and beat against that house; yet it did not fall, because it had its foundation on the rock.

MATTHEW 7:24–25

When you build a tower, what's the most important part of your structure? Is it the roof? The walls? The foundation—the very bottom of the building that's strong underneath the ground—is the most important part of any building project. Before a real-life builder even lays the first brick, he digs down deep into the soil and pours cement so the building will have something strong to stand on.

Jesus talked about your life having a foundation too. He said that when you put your trust in him, he'll help you stand tall and strong—even when life gets tough. You don't have to worry about being blown away by your problems when Jesus is taking care of you. When you put your faith in him, he'll never let you down.

Thank you, Jesus, for being my firm foundation. Help me remember when things get tough that you'll help me stand strong. I love you. Amen.

Destination: Kindness

Keep on loving one another as brothers and sisters.
HEBREWS 13:1

When you're going on a road trip to someplace new, your parents don't just get in the car and start driving in any direction. First, they probably plug in their phone or GPS and tell it where they want to go.

When you think about the kind of person Jesus wants you to be—kind, compassionate, and caring—you can get up every day and hope you're becoming more and more like that, or you can plan how you're going to get there.

What are some ways you can get to your goal of being kind, compassionate, and caring? Make a list of three things you can do. It might be not losing your temper so often with your brother, listening better when your friend has a problem, and doing something nice when your parents have had a long day. Whatever it is, you can get there with God's help.

Dear God, help me to be more kind, compassionate, and caring. Show me some little ways I can plan to love others. In Jesus' name, amen.

He'll Catch You

To you They cried ouT and were saved; in you They TrusTed and were noT puT To shame.

PSALM 22:5

When you think about your best friend, would you say that you trust her? What if she held out her arms and asked you to fall into them—backwards? Could you really count on your friend to catch you?

God says he will always catch you when you fall. He's not talking about when you trip over your feet at school—he's talking about when life gets tough and it feels like there's no one who can help. He's better than having a human friend there to catch you—he was powerful enough to create the whole world, so he's definitely powerful enough to help you through a hard time.

What's bugging you today? School problems? Friend or family problems? Does it feel like you have no one you can trust? Fall on Jesus by praying—ask him to help you, and he will—just like he promised.

Dear God, help me to trust you when life is tough. I can always fall on you, even when others let me down. I know that you can handle any problems I have. In Jesus' name, amen.

DAY 265

Miracles

For you created my inmost being; you knit me together in my mother's womb.

PSALM 139:13

When Jesus was on earth, he performed miracles. Groups of people crowded around him hoping to see what he would do next. He healed the sick, turned water into wine, walked on water—and so much more.

You might think you've never seen a miracle, but you actually have. Did you know that *you're* a miracle? Every part of you from your head to your toes is miraculous. There's no way you could exist without an amazing God creating you. The Bible says he knit you together in your mother's belly! Every life he makes is unexplainable. Every person you see today is God's awesome work. So next time you're tempted to wish you could see God do something miraculous, just look in the mirror. You're a walking, talking miracle.

Dear God, thank you for creating people as your miracles. Everything in your creation shows us how powerful you are. I love you. Amen.

When You Feel Judged

The woman said, 'I know that Messiah' (called Christ) 'is coming.
When he comes, he will explain everything to us.' Then Jesus
declared, 'I, the one speaking to you—I am he.'

JOHN 4:25–26

Once, when Jesus was on a journey, he made a special stop to talk to a woman who needed him. This lady was standing at the city's well, collecting water. She might've been there in the hottest part of the day because she didn't want to run into anyone else from her village—she'd made some bad decisions that other people judged her for.

When Jesus saw her, he told her that he knew about her sin and wanted to forgive her. Jesus sees your sin, too, and wants to forgive you. Even when others judge you or you feel ashamed, you can know that Jesus knows about your decisions and loves you still. Nothing can shake his love for you—not even the opinions of other people.

Dear Jesus, even when I feel judged by other people, I know that you see my sin and want to forgive me. Help me to accept your forgiveness and live for you. In Jesus' name, amen.

Does It Feel Impossible?

March around The ciTy once wiTh aLL The armed men. Do This for
six days . . . On The seventh day, march around The ciTy seven
Times, wiTh The priests bLowing The Trumpets.

JOSHUA 6:3, 4B

God wanted to help his people take over the city of Jericho, but first he told them they had to do something that seemed a little silly: walk in circles around the city for seven days. They were just supposed to walk— not run and not attack the city walls—not do anything that made them feel powerful. After the seventh time around the city, God told them to shout, and he brought the walls down to the ground. They simply fell without any other explanation.

Sometimes, like God's people at Jericho, you'll face something that seems impossible. God loves to do impossible things. But sometimes he wants to do them without anyone else taking the credit. Is there a problem in your life that you can't control? Trust God. He will work for your good even when you feel powerless. When he does something amazing, he gets the credit and you get to give him thanks.

Dear God, even when my problems are too big for me to handle, I know I can trust you. Thank you for the amazing things you can do. I give you the credit! In Jesus' name, amen.

Don't Do That One Thing

"You will not certainly die," the serpent said to the woman. "For God knows that when you eat from it your eyes will be opened, and you will be like God, knowing good and evil."
GENESIS 3:4-5

Have you ever wanted to do something you knew was wrong? Adam and Eve felt that way—Satan tempted them to do the one thing God had told them not to do—eat from the tree of the knowledge of good and evil.

Satan doesn't have any new tricks—he'll try to use the same one on you he used on Adam and Eve. He'll tempt you to do the one thing you know you're not supposed to do. When you want to tell your parents you're hanging out with your best friend but you go to a party instead, when you want to cheat on a test, and when you want to be mean to your brother or sister, that's Satan trying to trick you.

Since Satan's tricks aren't new, you know how to watch out for them. Next time you're tempted to do something you know you're not supposed to do, stand strong. You don't have to fall for your enemy's lies.

Dear God, help me to be smart about Satan's tricks. Help me to obey you because you want the best for me. Thank you for protecting me from my enemy's lies. In Jesus' name, amen.

A Greedy Guy

Ahab said to Naboth, "Let me have your vineyard to use for a vegetable garden, since it is close to my palace. In exchange I will give you a better vineyard or, if you prefer, I will pay you whatever it is worth." But Naboth replied, "The Lord forbid that I should give you the inheritance of my ancestors."

I Kings 21:2-3

Have you ever wanted something so badly that you felt like you would do anything to get it? There was a king named Ahab who had everything a person could ever want—he owned an entire kingdom. But outside of his window he could see a vineyard that belonged to a man named Naboth, and soon the king decided he would do anything to get it. Before long, Ahab and his wife decided to kill Naboth so they could have the land.

King Ahab's greed made him forget how important Naboth's life was. Nothing you could ever own is worth hurting someone for. When you're tempted to take something from someone else, stop to think about how it will affect the other person. Will they be sad? Angry? People are always more important than things, and you can show them that by respecting what they own.

Dear God, help me to always put people before things. Help me to be content with what I have, and not be jealous of others. You've given me all I need to be happy. In Jesus' name, amen.

Don't Stop Asking

So in The course of Time Hannah became pregnant and gave birth To a son. She named him Samuel, saying, "Because I asked The Lord for him."

1 Samuel 1:20

Hannah was very sad because she couldn't have a child. She prayed and prayed for God to give her a baby, but it didn't happen. Other women teased Hannah because she couldn't have children, and that made Hannah even sadder. Even when she was discouraged, she kept on praying and asking God for a child.

When you're praying and God doesn't seem to answer your prayer, don't give up. He might not say yes right away—Hannah needed to wait, and you might need to wait for what you want too. You're learning to trust God while you're waiting for his answer. When Hannah finally had a son, she knew that God had heard her all along. Don't give up just because your prayers don't seem to be answered right away. God hears you and he's working for your good.

Thank you, God, that you hear my prayers even when I feel like I'm waiting for answers. Thank you for taking care of me and giving me what's best. In Jesus' name, amen.

277

Using Your Words

Gracious words are a honeycomb, sweet to the soul and healing to the bones.

PROVERBS 16:24

We're all born knowing how to ask for what we want. When you were a baby, you couldn't use your words so you used your lungs to yell for what you needed. Now that you're older, you know how to say what you need. Sometimes you might feel embarrassed or shy about asking for help with something, but using your words works better than acting out.

If you're feeling so frustrated with your homework assignment that you want to toss the book across the room, ask your parents for help instead. Say something like, "This assignment is really frustrating me because I don't understand it. Can you explain it to me, please?" When you feel angry because your brother always gets the shower first, ask him if you can make a schedule and take turns.

It's normal to feel frustrated and even angry sometimes. When you start feeling that way, take a deep breath and think about which words you can use to help solve your problem. Using your words helps you feel better and may help your problem get better too.

Dear God, thank you for giving me the gift of words. Help me use them when I'm feeling upset or angry. I want to solve my problems by using words instead of acting out. In Jesus' name, amen.

DAY 272

Controlling?

'Eat and drink,' he says to you, but his heart is not with you.
PROVERBS 23:7B

Have you ever had a friend who tried to control you? Maybe he really wants what is in your lunch box, so he keeps begging for it until you give in. Or he really wants you to come to a bad movie, so he tells your parents that you are just going on a sleepover.

It's no fun when someone else tries to control you. When a friend starts acting that way, it's a good idea to stand up to that person and say no. You can say, "I don't like it when someone tries to control me," or, "I don't like how what you're doing is making me feel." When you tell your friend you're not willing to be manipulated, you're taking a stand for yourself. You don't have to give in just because someone else wants you to—you can be your own person!

Dear God, thank you for making me my own person and that I don't have to let anyone manipulate me. Thank you for helping me make decisions for myself! I love you. In Jesus' name, amen.

Filling Your Tank

Everything that lives and moves about will be food for you. Just as I gave you the green plants, I now give you everything.

GENESIS 9:3

Have you ever seen your mom fill her car's gas tank up with sugar water? Or watched her pour chocolate in it? Do you think her car would go very far if she put cheese in the gas tank? Of course not! Most cars are designed to run on one type of fuel.

Did you know your body is made to run on a special type of fuel too? The plants, animals, and water in nature are all things God created that can help your body go. Sometimes it's fun to have a special treat like cake or cookies, but when you eat too much of that treat it can leave you feeling sick or even sad. Treats are just that: treats! God gave you a special body with special needs. Take care of your body by eating healthy and it will get you where you want to go.

Dear God, help me put good fuel into my body. I want to keep myself healthy and strong. Thank you for giving me the right kinds of food so I can do that. In Jesus' name, amen.

Staying Positive

May These words of my mouth and This meditation of my heart
be pleasing in your sight, LORD, my Rock and my Redeemer.
PSALM 19:14

Sometimes when you're having a bad day, it's hard to stay positive. But did you know that when you try to think happy thoughts, those thoughts can help you figure out how to fix whatever's bothering you? Thinking happy thoughts is like standing on top of a lookout tower: every positive thought lifts you higher, and pretty soon you can see your problems more clearly and come up with ways to solve them.

Have you been fighting with a friend? Take a few minutes to close your eyes and think about all the good memories you have with him or her. Is your homework really hard today? Write out a list of all the ways this school subject will help you in life. Practice thinking positive thoughts when you're feeling discouraged. Those thoughts will be the boost you need to solve your problems and feel happy again.

Dear God, help me remember to stay positive on days when a problem is discouraging me. Thank you for those happy thoughts that will help me figure out what to do so I can feel better again. In Jesus' name, amen.

God's Ways or the World's Ways?

"For my thoughts are not your thoughts, neither are your ways my ways," declares the Lord.

ISAIAH 55:8

Have you ever noticed how God's ways sometimes seem backwards from the world's ways? The world will tell you to take revenge on someone who has hurt you, but God will tell you to forgive that person. The world will tell you to brag about what you've accomplished, but God will tell you to thank him for all he's helped you do.

Sometimes it's easy to forget God's ways, and listen to what the people in the world are telling you. That's why it's important to spend time with God every single day. When you hear his word and hide it in your heart, you'll become the person he wants you to be—not forgetting that God's ways are so much better than the world's.

Dear God, thank you for doing things backwards from the world when you sent Jesus to die for my sin. Help me to do things the right way for you instead of listening to the lies the world tries to tell me. I want to make a difference for you. In Jesus' name, amen.

Your Body

Rather, it should be that of your inner self, the unfading beauty of a gentle and quiet spirit, which is of great worth in God's sight.

1 PETER 3:4

Some people are going to say you're too tall or too short, your eye color is wrong, or your hair color looks silly. No matter what you look like, some people will always find a reason to pick on you.

God says you're perfect in every way. He likes the way you look because he made you that way. Before he made the whole world, he already had in mind exactly what he wanted you to look like. When others pick on you, it makes him sad because he knows you are amazing. No matter what other people say, you should always remember that God loves you just the way you are. He thinks you're perfect, and that's all that matters.

Thank you, God, for making my body just the way it is on purpose. If others pick on me for how I look, I know that I'm perfectly loved and accepted by you. In Jesus' name, amen.

Asking for Directions

The Israelites sampled their provisions but did not inquire of the
Lord. Then Joshua made a treaty of peace with them to let them
live, and the leaders of the assembly ratified it by oath.
JOSHUA 9:14–15

God told Joshua and the army of Israel to claim all the land around them as theirs. When their army began to win wars against other nations, the Gibeonites heard about God's powerful army and decided to trick Joshua. They packed moldy bread and wore old shoes, then told Joshua that they were from a faraway country (they were from nearby) and wanted the Israelites to promise not to make war with them. Without asking God, Joshua and the Israelites promised to keep peace with the Gibeonites.

When we forget to ask God for direction, sometimes we make poor choices like the Israelites did. God is always waiting to give us wisdom about our decisions but only if we ask. Next time you're about to make a decision, pause and ask God for direction. Through his Word and the advice of Christian adults, God will help you figure out what you need to do, and you'll not be tricked like the Israelites.

Dear God, help me remember to ask you about the decisions in my life. Thank you for always being there and helping me make good choices. In Jesus' name, amen.

DAY 278

Are They Lying?

The woman whose son was alive was deeply moved out of love for her son and said to the king, "Please, my Lord, give her the living baby! Don't kill him!"

1 Kings 3:26a

Two women came to King Solomon and asked for his help. The ladies lived together and both had had a baby—but one of the babies had died. Both women wanted the living baby for herself. King Solomon told the women that he could cut the baby in half and give one half to each woman. He wasn't really going to do that—he was testing them. One woman begged him not to kill the child, and the other one told him to go ahead and kill the baby. The king knew that the woman who wanted to protect the baby was its mother. She wanted the best for the child.

Sometimes, someone may tell you a lie. You might get a strange feeling about what that person is saying to you, and it might be hard to be sure if they're being honest. When you think someone might be lying to you, ask God to help you figure it out. He'll give you wisdom and show you what to do.

Dear God, help me have the wisdom to tell the truth from a lie. You're the only one who can help me see when someone's trying to be tricky. Thank you for always being there to show me the truth. In Jesus' name, amen.

The Bronze Snake

JUST as Moses lifTed up The snake in The wilderness, so The Son of Man must be lifTed up, ThaT everyone who believes may have eTernal life in him.

JOHN 3:14–15

When the Israelites were traveling through the wilderness, there were a lot of poisonous snakes that kept biting people. There were no hospitals or medicine back then, so Moses asked God what to do. God told Moses to lift up a sign with a bronze snake on a pole, and whoever was bitten by a snake looked at the bronze snake and was healed.

Jesus is like that sign for us—our sin is like a poison that we can't save ourselves from. But Jesus was lifted up on a cross so that we can call out to him and be saved. No one else the Israelites called out to would have saved them from the poison, and no one else we call out to can save us from our sin. No matter what anyone else tries to tell you, the Bible says Jesus is the only way. Have you asked him to forgive your sin?

Dear God, thank you for sending Jesus so that I could be forgiven from my sin. Thank you for making this the only way so that I know how to be saved. I love you. In Jesus' name, amen.

Endless Oil

For This is What The Lord, The God of Israel, says: 'The jar of
flour will not be used up and The jug of oil will not run dry until
The day The Lord sends rain on The land.'

1 Kings 17:14

Elijah was visiting a town called Zaraphath, and he had nothing to eat.
He met a widow, and asked her for some food. She told him she didn't
have any bread because there hadn't been any rain for food to
grow—she only had a little bit of oil and flour, and she and her
son were about to eat it as their last meal and then die. Elijah
promised the woman she wouldn't run out of food if she gave
him something to eat. She believed him and fed him first.
What Elijah said was true—the woman didn't run out of oil
or flour in her jars until it rained and food grew again.

When you see someone in need, you can give to them no matter how
much or how little you have. When you share with others, God promises
he'll provide for your needs too. You're his child, and he's not going to let
you go without. It's important to share with others what God has shared
with you!

Dear God, thank you for providing what I need. Help me remember to
share with others, even when it means I might not get as much for myself.
Thank you for taking care of all your children. In Jesus' name, amen.

He Came for You

For God so loved the world that he gave his one and only
Son, that whoever believes in him shall not perish but have
eternal life.

JOHN 3:16

When Jesus was born, God put a star in the sky to tell some wise men
that a new king had come. He sent angels to tell shepherds the same
thing. Imagine—from people living in castles to people living outside—
God wanted *all* people to know he'd sent his son for everyone.

You don't have to feel important (even though you are!) to know that
Jesus came for you. You could live in a huge house or a tiny apartment.
You could wear name brand or off brand clothes. You could go to the
newest school or the oldest school. It doesn't matter what you own or
what your social status is—Jesus came for you. When he looks at you, he
sees your heart—not your wallet. You're important to God, and because
of that, Jesus came to save you.

Dear God, thank you for sending Jesus for me. No matter how much I
have, you think I'm important. In Jesus' name, amen.

Suffering for Jesus

Continue to remember those in prison as if you were together with them in prison, and those who are mistreated as if you yourselves were suffering.

HEBREWS 13:3

One of the saddest stories in the Bible is when people threw stones at a man named Stephen because he believed in Jesus. As he was dying, Stephen looked up and saw the sky opening and God welcoming him to his heavenly home. God hadn't forgotten Stephen—Stephen's bravery would encourage many people to believe in Jesus too.

There are people around the world who, like Stephen, are suffering for Jesus. The Bible tells us that we should remember to pray for those people around the world who are being persecuted for Jesus. We don't have to know their names—God knows who they are, and our prayers make a difference in their lives. As we pray for those who are suffering, their bravery can help give us courage to stand up for Jesus too.

Dear God, I pray for my brothers and sisters in Jesus who are suffering because of their faith. Give them bravery and hope. Thank you for helping them stand strong for you and heal their suffering. In Jesus' name, amen.

The Unmerciful Servant

BuT when ThaT servanT wenT ouT, he found one of his fellow servants who owed him a hundred silver coins. He grabbed him and began To choke him. 'Pay back whaT you owe me!' he demanded.

MATTHEW 18:28

Jesus told a parable about a servant who owed his master a lot of money—more money than he could repay in a lifetime. The man threw himself at his master's feet and begged for more time to repay his debt.

The master felt bad for his servant and forgave him the entire amount. Then the servant went that same day and threw someone else in prison for not paying him a much smaller amount.

The Bible says the servant who didn't forgive the debt is like us when we don't forgive. God is like the master who did forgive. When we refuse to forgive someone it's like we've forgotten how much God has forgiven us. Is there someone you can forgive today?

Dear God, help me to be willing to forgive others because of how much you've forgiven me. When I forgive someone, I don't just set them free from their debt—I set myself free from holding a grudge. I love you. In Jesus' name, amen.

DAY 284

His Will

Your kingdom come, your will be done, on earth as it is in heaven.
MATTHEW 6:10

When Jesus was teaching one day, he gave an example of how to pray. While he was praying he told God, "Thy kingdom come, thy will be done." He was showing that when you pray to God, you should start out by asking for God's will to be done, not yours.

Sometimes God's will is going to be the same as yours, and sometimes it isn't. You might pray for a friend who needs to be saved, and that's something God wants too. You might pray for a friend to be healed, but God might have other plans for your friend. It's good to tell God whatever you're feeling when you pray, but it's also important to accept his will. When you pray and ask for what he wants, he'll help you understand that he knows best.

Dear God, thank you for being all-knowing, and that I don't have to understand your will. Thank you for helping me pray for what you want—you want the best for me. In Jesus' name, amen.

291

DAY 285

Hidden Treasure

The Lord looks down from heaven on all mankind To see if There are any who understand, any who seek God.

PSALM 14:2

If you're looking for something important, do you keep looking until you find it? Maybe you're looking for the perfect present for your friend's birthday, or for a clue on a scavenger hunt, or for the perfect after-school hangout.

When you spend your time looking for God, it shows how important he is to you. You can look for him in the Bible, when you read it every day. In prayer, both at home and at church. And you can look for him in nature, because he created every amazing thing you see. Proof of God is everywhere, but you have to take the time to search for him like the treasure he is. What are some ways you plan to look for God today?

Dear God, you're a treasure worth searching for. Help me remember to look for you in my every-day life. I love you. In Jesus' name, amen.

The Curtain Torn in Two

AT That moment The curtain of The TempLe was Torn in Two from
Top To boTTom.

MATTHEW 27:51A

Before Jesus came to take our sin, God's people were not allowed to come into his presence because he was so holy and perfect. Once a year when his people were confessing their sin, a priest would go into a special room in the temple, called the Holy of Holies, to offer a sacrifice so the people could be forgiven. The room was separated from the rest of the temple by a large curtain.

When Jesus died on the cross, the curtain between the Holy of Holies and the rest of the temple ripped in half. This was God's way of showing that because Jesus took the punishment for our sin we could now be in his presence any time. Our sin no longer keeps us from approaching God—we can talk to him anytime, anywhere. That's a blessing we can't imagine! Have you talked with God today?

Dear God, thank you for inviting me into your presence any time. Thank you for sending Jesus so that my sin will not stand in the way of knowing you. I love you. In Jesus' name, amen.

A Strange Guy

John's clothes were made of camel's hair, and he had a leather belt round his waist. His food was locusts and wild honey.

MATTHEW 3:4

John the Baptist had a special job—tell others that the Savior was on his way. Huge crowds went to hear John speak, but some people thought he was weird because he lived in the wilderness, ate locusts, and dressed a little funny.

It's hard not to judge people based on what you see with your eyes. Someone might live in a different place than you do, eat different things, and dress differently. You might feel tempted to think you're better than another person, but God has a special plan for that person's life too. No matter where someone lives, what they eat, or how they dress—always remind yourself that God works through all types of people. Look at what he did through John the Baptist!

Dear God, help me to see others the way you see them—special creations made for special purposes. Thank you for having a special plan for me too. In Jesus' name, amen.

Lend a Hand

Religion that God our Father accepts as pure and faultless is this:
To look after orphans and widows in their distress and to keep
oneself from being polluted by the world.

JAMES 1:27

Did you know that God especially looks out for people who can't take care of themselves? The Bible talks about people who are dependent on others to care for them—older people, sick people, and kids without parents are all under his care—and he wants to use you to take care of those people.

Do you know an older person you can help with house-work? Someone who's sick and needs food brought to them? You could even send some of your chore money to an organization that takes care of orphans around the world. It's an adventure to love the people God loves. Ask your parents if there's someone they know whom you could reach out to together. You could make a huge difference in someone's life by loving them like Jesus.

Dear God, help me keep my eyes open for people who can't take care of themselves. Give me ideas of how I can help those people and love them like you do. In Jesus' name, amen.

295

Who's My Family?

He replied, 'My mother and brothers are those who hear God's word and put it into practice.'

LUKE 8:21

When Jesus was teaching one day, his mother and brothers came to see him. The crowd was so big that his family couldn't get near him. When Jesus' disciples told him that his family was trying to see him, Jesus said, "My mother and brothers are those who hear God's Word and put it into practice." Jesus was saying that anyone who loves God was also a part of his family. That means Jesus treats anyone in God's family with the same love as he would the family he was born into.

You can treat others in God's family with the same love you would your own family. Would you be sad for your brother if someone bullied him? You can also feel bad for a friend at church who's having a hard time. What about doing something nice for your mom if she had a bad day? You could do something kind for someone at church when they're having a bad day too. Now that you know Jesus, you don't have just one small family—you have a huge family you can love.

Dear God, help me remember that my church friends are also my family. Help me treat them well and love them like I would my own family. In Jesus' name, amen.

No Match for Jesus

He said to them, 'Go!' So they came out and went into the pigs,
and the whole herd rushed down the steep bank into the lake and
died in the water.

MATTHEW 8:32

When Jesus was walking through the countryside one day, two men who had many demons living inside them came near. Jesus felt sorry for the men and told the demons they had to leave the men alone. The demons that had bothered the men for so long left immediately—they were no match for Jesus.

Your problems are no match for Jesus, either. He is bigger and stronger than whatever's bothering you—family, school, or friend problems. You might feel like there's no way things could get better, but that isn't true. The same Jesus who took care of the demon-possessed men promises to take care of you. He might not send your problems running away, but he will give you strength until those problems are gone. You are special to Jesus, and he's powerful enough to take care of you.

Dear God, thank you for being so powerful. Thank you for helping my problems get better, and helping me be strong until they do. In Jesus' name, amen.

How's Your Appetite?

Blessed are those who hunger and thirst for righteousness, for they shall be filled.

MATTHEW 5:6

When you eat a lot of junk food, your tummy gets full and you don't always have room for the important stuff. Pizza, ice cream, and potato chips are okay every once in a while—but when you don't leave room for fruits and vegetables, your body might not get the vitamins it needs to stay healthy.

Did you know there's such a thing as having a healthy appetite for God too? Just like your body can get full on junk food, your spirit can get full on junk. Going to the movies and watching television aren't bad things to do—but when you fill your time with just entertainment, you might not feel like making time to read your Bible and pray. If you feel like you're not interested in spending time with God, try cutting back on how many video games you play and how much television you watch. Then use that time to fill your mind and heart with the good stuff that will make you healthy and strong.

Dear God, help me have a healthy appetite for spending time with you. I know it's your Word that will help me become the best person I can be. In Jesus' name, amen.

He'll Complete It

Being confident of this, that he who began a good work in you
will carry it on to completion until the day of Christ Jesus.
PHILIPPIANS 1:6

When you're making something awesome, have you ever stopped in the middle and forgotten about it? You might build half a model airplane, paint half a picture, or write half a short story. God doesn't stop in the middle of what he's doing, though, or we might only have half a world!

When you came to know Jesus, God began to create something amazing in your heart. With every day that goes by he keeps building new things in you. He's helping you become more patient, more kind, and loving. With every day that passes, he is making you more like him—and that's worth the wait. God won't quit in the middle of his work—he'll finish it someday. So next time you're feeling impatient with yourself for messing up, remember God's still working on you. He won't stop until you're with him and he's finished!

Dear God, thanks for not giving up on me. Thanks for building something amazing in me! Help me to be patient and to help you as you create new things in me. In Jesus' name, amen.

At War

For The flesh desires whaT is conTrary To The SpiriT, and The SpiriT whaT is conTrary To The flesh. They are in conflicT wiTh each oTher, so ThaT you are noT To do whaTever you wanT.

GALATIANS 5:17

Have you ever watched a cartoon where the devil's standing on one shoulder and an angel's standing on the other shoulder of a character? The devil and the angel are both trying to convince the person to do something—they're usually at war with each other.

The apostle Paul said he was at war with his own flesh. In other words, his human nature wanted to do things that were wrong, but God's spirit was telling him to do things that were right. Have you ever felt that way? Maybe you were tempted to look at your classmate's test, but your heart told you it was the wrong choice. Or you felt like sneaking dessert out of the pantry, but your heart told you it wasn't a good idea. Until you get to heaven, you'll always be tempted to do wrong things. The more you practice saying "no" to your human nature, though, the better you'll be at it. God's spirit is stronger than your human nature and can help you make the right choice.

Dear God, help me to listen to your spirit when I'm tempted to do the wrong thing. Thank you for helping me say no to sin and yes to you! In Jesus' name, amen.

A Friend Who Tells the Truth

Wounds from a friend can be trusted, but an enemy
multiplies kisses.

PROVERBS 27:6

If you were walking around with a hole in your shorts, would you want a friend to tell you, or would you rather they let you get embarrassed? Sometimes an honest friend can save you from getting hurt.

The Bible says a true friend doesn't just agree with everything you say or do—a true friend will be honest with you because they care and want you to be okay. A friend may tell you that you shouldn't lie to your parents, and it might not feel good to hear. A friend may ask you to be kinder to someone at school, and you might feel a little mad at first. But God says a friend who's honest with you in a loving way is a special person—you've found someone you can really trust. And a true friend is hard to find.

Dear God, thank you for any true friend you've put in my life. Help me be willing to hear the hard things. Thank you for being a true friend to me too. In Jesus' name, amen.

DAY 295

Refiner's Fire

For you, God, tested us; you refined us like silver.
PSALM 66:10

Before a silversmith makes jewelry, he has to clean the gold. If he doesn't use completely pure silver, the piece of jewelry will become weak and break. There's only one way to get the silver completely clean—he has to heat it up so hot that it turns into liquid before it cools and hardens again.

God says he's like a silversmith, and you're his precious gold. Sometimes he allows problems in your life that are going to feel a lot like that hot stove—very uncomfortable. Those problems might not feel good, but God's using them to make you into a stronger person. Like a silversmith making a beautiful piece of jewelry, God's making something beautiful out of your life. You can trust him even when things get uncomfortable.

Dear God, thank you for treating me like valuable gold. I know that you're taking care of me and making me stronger through my problems—help me to trust you, even when I don't see your work. In Jesus' name, amen.

No Longer a Slave

Perhaps the reason he was separated from you for a little while was that you might have him back forever—no longer as a slave, but better than a slave, as a dear brother.
PHILEMON 1:15–16A

There was a man named Onesimus who was a slave in the house of a guy named Philemon. One day, Onesimus escaped from Philemon's house and ran away to another city. When he got to the city, he met the apostle Paul and became a Christian. Onesimus told Paul about his former master, so Paul wrote a letter to Philemon. He explained that Onesimus shouldn't be treated as a slave but as a brother.

Is there someone in your life you're not treating like a brother or sister? Maybe you expect that person to do things for you, but you don't treat them like you care. When someone helps you, it should be because of their kindness—not because they feel like they *have to*. What ways can you show kindness to others?

Dear God, help me treat others with kindness … like they're my brother or sister. Help me not to take my friends and family for granted but to appreciate what they do for me. In Jesus' name, amen.

Better Than Christmas

And I will dwell in the house of the LORD forever.
PSALM 23:6B

Have you ever counted down the days to something you're looking forward to? It might be Christmas, your birthday, or a special vacation. Maybe you're ready for school to start or you're ready to get out on summer break. Whatever you're excited about, you know exactly how long it will be until it happens. You also know the disappointment you feel when what you've been looking forward to is over too quickly.

One of the awesome things about heaven is that it isn't something that comes and goes. You'll get to spend forever in an amazing place where you'll never be bored. Going there is better than any Christmas, birthday, or vacation you'll ever experience. And you don't have to worry about going back to normal life! God is a wonderful God to give you this amazing home where you can stay forever!

Dear God, thank you for giving me a place I can look forward to—a place where I'll never be bored and I'll never have to worry about leaving. Thank you for loving me enough to create a place for me. In Jesus' name, amen.

DAY 298

Another Kind of Healthy

Above all else, guard your heart, for everything you do flows from it.

PROVERBS 4:23

You know that to take care of your body you should eat right, exercise, and get enough sleep. What about taking care of your emotions— the feelings you have? Doing things to help your emotions stay steady is called emotional health.

Some of the things you do to take care of your emotional health are the same as what you do to take care of your body. Eating right, exercising, and getting enough sleep can all help you feel happy. Some other ways you can take care of your emotional health are picking positive friends, keeping up with your homework so you're not stressed, and even going to church so you feel more connected to God and others who share your beliefs and your faith. Finding an adult or a good friend to talk with can help too.

Taking care of your body is a wonderful thing, but so is taking care of your emotional health. What's one thing you can do to help achieve that goal today?

Dear God, thank you for giving me the gift of emotions—feelings. Help me to take care of my emotional health. In Jesus' name, amen.

When Friends Doubt

Be merciful to those who doubt.
JUDE 1:22

When you're going through a hard time, would you rather have someone tell you to cheer up, or would you rather they tell you that they've been there and they understand? It always feels good when someone tells you they understand what you're going through.

It's important to understand and care about people who feel doubt about God's goodness. There may come a time when something difficult happens to one of your Christian friends, and that friend might feel like God isn't good or he isn't with them. Instead of judging that person for their doubts, think about how you'd feel in their shoes. Ask if there's anything you can do to help and then pray for them. When you show mercy to someone who feels doubt, you're being like Jesus to that person—and that could make all the difference in their faith.

Dear God, thank you for being merciful to me when I'm feeling doubts about your goodness. Help me to show that same mercy to others when they're feeling doubts. In Jesus' name, amen.

His Heart or His Hand?

Look To The Lord and his strength; seek his face always.
I CHRONICLES 16:11

What if your mom served you dinner and you grabbed it right out of her hands without looking into her eyes to say thanks? What if your teacher handed you your assignment and you grunted at her or your brother or sister helped you with your homework and you told them you didn't want to hang out with them? Your mom, your teacher, and your sibling would probably feel like you didn't care about them—you only care about what they can do for you.

When you pray, remember to not just ask God for what you need. Take time to thank him for what he's already done. God doesn't want to just bless you with good things—he wants to bless you with himself. He loves you and wants you to know him, not just his good gifts.

Dear God, help me remember that the greatest gift you give me is time with you. Thank you for the other blessings you give me too. Help me remember to hang out with you every chance I get. In Jesus' name, amen.

Being Kind to Pets

The righteous care for the needs of their animals, but the kindest acts of the wicked are cruel.

PROVERBS 12:10

Have you ever looked into a dog's eyes and noticed how he asked for attention? Have you ever heard a cat purr as a thank-you or hiss as a warning? Whether you're a dog lover, a cat lover, or not an animal person—you can still be kind to the creatures God put on this earth.

Animals don't have words, so they count on us to help take care of them. If you have a pet at home, it might be your job to feed that pet or let him outside. This is an important job—that pet is relying on your help. If you get up first thing in the morning to feed yourself, you can feed your pet too. Give him a pat on the head (or some food in the bowl if he's a fish) before you go to bed. If you don't have a pet but your friend does, you can pay attention to their pet when you go to your friend's house. A little bit of love goes a long way, and you're showing a kind heart by caring for the animal God put in your life.

Dear God, help me to be kind to the animals you've put in my life. Help me never to mistreat another creature just because it's smaller than me. Thank you for caring for me even though I'm smaller than you. In Jesus' name, amen.

Scary Dreams

When I am afraid, I put my TrusT in you.
PSALM 56:3

It happens sometimes—you're fast asleep when all of a sudden you wake up with your heart pounding, your body sweating, and your mind replaying a bad dream. You're probably a little relieved to wake up and realize it was just a dream, but it can still be a scary feeling.

What can you do when you have a bad dream that just won't leave you alone? You can pray to God about it. In the Bible, lots of people prayed about their dreams. God cares about everything that happens in your life—even the things that wake you up at night. If you find you're having bad dreams a lot, maybe you could talk with your parents or a friend about how to feel less stressed. God is bigger than your dreams and he can help you find the peace you need.

Dear God, when I have a bad dream, help me remember that you're bigger than that dream. Give me peace to fall asleep again with good thoughts of you and your kindness. In Jesus' name, amen

Feeling Jealous

Whoever claims to love God yet hates a brother or sister is a liar.
For whoever does not love their brother and sister, whom they
have seen, cannot love God, whom they have not seen.
I JOHN 4:20

Everyone feels jealous sometimes—it's a normal emotion. But do you find yourself feeling jealous a lot? Maybe it's your brother or your sister or someone at church. That person might get more attention, have more money, or go to more fun places than you.

When you start feeling jealous of someone, you might also start feeling tempted to make things worse for the other person. If you think about it for long enough, your mind will try to come up with ways to make sure your sibling or cousin doesn't get treated better than you. But it's important to remember that God doesn't treat anyone with favoritism. Even when your family member seems like they're getting more attention, God doesn't see that person as any better than you. Next time you get jealous, try respectfully telling your parents or other family what you're feeling. Even if nothing changes, remember that God sees you and loves you every bit as much as anyone.

Dear God, thank you for loving me as much as you love the other members of my family. Help me not to be upset if someone seems to get more attention than I do. In Jesus' name, amen.

Prayer Works

Suddenly an angel of The Lord appeared and a Light Shone in The cell. He Struck Peter on The Side and woke him up. "Quick, geT up!" he said, and The chains fell off PeTer's wrisTs.

ACTS 12:7

Have you ever noticed the glass doors in the front of big buildings? All you have to do is step on the sensor and the doors will slide open to let you outside. That's what happened to Peter one night when he was in prison for standing up for Jesus—except the doors weren't electric and they weren't supposed to let prisoners outside! God had miraculously opened the gate to let Peter escape.

Paul's church friends were holding a prayer meeting for him when he got out of prison. God had answered their prayers, allowing Peter to escape. God can answer your prayers in big ways too. When you ask him to help someone you love, you never know what kind of miracle he might send. He's a big God who can open big doors!

Dear God, thank you for answering my prayers in amazing ways. Help me to trust your answer when it's yes—and help me to respect your answer when it's no. Thank you for knowing what's best for me and the people I love! In Jesus' name, amen.

Clothes Matter

The Lord God made garments of skin for Adam and his wife and clothed Them.

GENESIS 3:21

Did you know that God made your body amazing, but parts of your body are only for you? Those parts are special parts that aren't meant to be shown to everyone. That's why people wear clothes—to cover up the private parts God made for your eyes only.

When you're picking out clothes, think about whether your clothes are going to cover the parts that are special to only you. Are your shorts so short that your underwear's showing? Are you following the dress code rules from your school, or the rules your parents make? Make sure you're dressing in a way that is comfortable and keeps you covered in all the right spots.

You have an incredible body that you should never be ashamed of. Take care of it by keeping the special parts for yourself, and not for other peoples' eyes. When you go shopping for clothes, you can find fun and stylish clothes that also do the important job of keeping you covered in all the right places!

Dear God, help me pick out clothes that show respect for the amazing body you gave me. In Jesus' name, amen.

DAY 306

Managing Money

Give to everyone what you owe them: if you owe taxes, pay taxes; if revenue, then revenue; if respect, then respect; if honor, then honor.

ROMANS 13:7-8

When you earn money, do you spend it all right away or do you save some? It's fun to buy new stuff, but it's also good to practice learning to save some of what you earn or what you're given. If you practice saving some of your money now, you'll know how to save when you're older.

Your mom or your dad get bills in the mail, and they have to set aside a certain amount of money each month to pay those bills. Some of their money goes to groceries, some to bills, and some to clothes and other expenses. Whatever is left over they can save for doing something fun later, or for emergencies. Having a little extra in the bank is always a good idea—you never know when you might need it!

Dear God, help me remember to put some of my money aside for important things. Thank you for giving me money for fun stuff and for things I might need. Help me to use it wisely. In Jesus' name, amen.

Finding God's Will

Therefore do not be foolish, but understand what the Lord's will is.
EPHESIANS 5:17

Have you ever had a decision to make, but you couldn't tell what God wanted you to do? Maybe you were trying to find a new friend, decide on a church to attend, or whether you should play sports this season. God has a lot of ways to help you figure out what to do.

One way is by praying to God. Another way is to read your Bible. And the third way is to ask people who are older and wiser than you. Even better, using all three of these ways together can help point you in the right direction. What kinds of decisions are you trying to make?

Dear God, help me remember to pray, read my Bible, and ask for wise advice when I'm trying to learn your will. Thank you for showing me exactly what I'm supposed to do and where I'm supposed to be. In Jesus' name, amen.

Your Inheritance

[The Holy Spirit] is a deposit guaranteeing our inheritance until
The redemption of those who are God's possession—to the praise
of his glory.

EPHESIANS 1:14

Sometimes when someone dies, they leave something called an inheritance for their family. These are possessions and they are divided up between the children or family of the person who passed away. An inheritance can be money, objects (like a painting or jewelry), or even homes.

When Jesus died and went back to heaven, he left the guarantee of an inheritance for us. He wanted us to know he was serious about coming back for us, so he left a promise. He didn't leave us money or houses—he left us something much better. He left us his Holy Spirit! The Holy Spirit comes to live inside of us when we trust Jesus as our savior. The Spirit tells us right from wrong, and teaches us how to pray. The best part is, our inheritance never leaves us—it's always with us. There's never been a better promise of our inheritance than the Holy Spirit!

Dear God, thank you for leaving the Holy Spirit for me as an inheritance. I can always depend on the Holy Spirit to be there for me. In Jesus' name, amen.

Your High Priest

For This reason he had To be made Like Them, fully human in every way, in order ThaT he mighT become a merciful and faiThful high priesT in service To God, and ThaT he mighT make aTonemenT for The sins of The people.

HEBREWS 2:17

In the Old Testament, there were priests who lived in the temple and offered sacrifices to God. These priests all had different jobs, but one priest was called a high priest—he was the leader. It was that priest's job to offer sacrifices for people so they would be forgiven from their sin.

In the New Testament, Jesus was called a high priest. Jesus was the son of God, but, like the high priests who came before him, Jesus was also human. Next time you think God might not understand what you're going through, remember Jesus was human too. He knows the temptations you face. He knows what you're going through. And he wants you to choose to follow him, even when that seems hard.

Dear God, thank you for sending Jesus—a high priest who understands when I'm tempted. Thank you for helping me make good choices. In Jesus' name, amen.

God Moves in Different Ways

"Sir," The invalid replied, "I have no one To help me inTo The pool when The water is sTirred. While I am Trying To geT in, someone else goes down ahead of me."

JOHN 5:7

Back in Bible days, there was a holy place called the Pool of Bethesda. According to some records, an angel would come to stir up the water in the pool, and the first person to jump in afterward would be healed of whatever sickness he had.

One day Jesus was standing beside the pool when he asked a man who couldn't walk if he'd like to be healed. The man explained to Jesus that he didn't have anyone to put him in the pool. He thought he had no chance of getting better. The man thought there was only one way for God to heal him—but God sent Jesus instead.

Sometimes God will do things in your life differently than you expect. You might think he only has one way to solve your problem, but he has something totally different in mind. When you get discouraged because God isn't fixing your problem the way you expect, remember the man by the Pool of Bethesda. God often works in ways you don't expect.

Dear God, thank you for helping solve my problems in ways I don't expect. Thank you for not being limited by the way I think things should be done. I trust you. In Jesus' name, amen.

Jesus Looks for You

For This is what The Sovereign Lord says: I myself will search for my sheep and look after them.

EZEKIEL 34:11

Doesn't it feel good when you're lonely and someone comes and finds you? Maybe when you're feeling sad, you hope your mom or dad will come into your room and ask you what's wrong and hug you. Maybe when you've scored the winning goal, you'd love for your coach to congratulate you for your hard work.

Those things might not always happen, but Jesus promises he's always checking on you. He always wants to be around you—he wants to hang out with you when you're feeling sad and let you know you're special. He loves you so much and he wants you to always feel like he cares.

Dear God, thank you for the assurance that when I'm feeling sad or just need attention, Jesus is there looking for me and looking after me. In Jesus' name, amen.

No Appearance of Evil

Reject every kind of evil.
I THESSALONIANS 5:22

Sometimes your friends might do something that you don't want to be a part of. They might want you to watch an inappropriate or violent movie, or offer you something you know you're not supposed to eat or drink. It's tough to walk away from that situation, but God says you should reject every kind of evil.

To reject every kind of evil means that no one would see you doing something bad with a group of friends and think you might be doing it too. That doesn't mean you can never hang out with your friends, it just means you find something else to do when they're doing something Christians aren't supposed to. That way, anyone who watches you will know you're doing your best to honor God. You won't be tempted to do something you know you're not supposed to.

Dear God, help me to reject every kind of evil. Help me to love my friends, but to also be careful about hanging out with them when they're doing things that don't honor you. In Jesus' name, amen.

You're God's Royal Family

BuT you are a chosen people, a royal priesThood, a holy nation,
God's special possession, ThaT you may declare The praises of him
who called you ouT of darkness inTo his wonderful LighT.
I PETER 2:9

Have you ever wished you were a part of a royal family? Maybe you've seen drawings of royalty in history books, or photos of a royal family in the checkout line at the grocery store. You imagine what it feels like to live in a castle and have ownership of an entire kingdom.

Did you know that you *are* royalty? You might not live in a castle or wear a crown, but God says because you belong to him, you're part of a royal family! That doesn't mean you get to demand what you want all the time, but it does mean that God thinks you're special. Jesus was royalty, too, but instead of acting stuck up or demanding, he treated everyone with kindness and respect. With his help, you can do the same thing as royalty!

Dear God, thank you for seeing me as part of your royal family. Help me treat others and myself the way that you treat me. In Jesus' name, amen.

He Gets You

He was despised and rejected by mankind, a man of suffering, and familiar with pain. Like one from whom people hide their faces he was despised, and we held him in low esteem.
ISAIAH 53:3

Has someone ever made fun of you or told you they don't like you? Maybe they wouldn't let you sit next to them on the bus, or they went out of their way to make sure no one played with you during P.E. A friend could have acted angry, or a bully at school could have been cruel.

When someone treats you unkindly, you might feel like no one else understands how much it hurts. The Bible says that even Jesus—who was perfect and never hurt anyone—knows what it's like for someone to be cruel. It's sad how people can be so mean sometimes. But like Jesus, you can keep being yourself and loving those who hurt you. Know that Jesus gets it—he understands what you're going through, and you're never alone.

Dear God, thank you for understanding how it feels when I'm hurting—and that I'm never alone. Help me know how to love others even when they're being unkind to me. In Jesus' name, amen.

You're Sealed By Him

Now it is God who makes both us and you stand firm in Christ. He anointed us, set his seal of ownership on us, and put his Spirit in our hearts as a deposit, guaranteeing what is to come.

2 CORINTHIANS 1:21-22

When a king sent out an important letter in Bible times, he sealed it with a special stamp and wax that showed the letter was from him. No one else had access to that stamp—everyone who read the letter could be sure that it was from the king, and that the letter contained important information.

God says he's marked your life with his own special seal. From the beginning of time, he made you for a reason. When others look at you, they can see that God's seal of ownership is on you—that you are going to make a difference for his kingdom. When life gets hard and you're not sure that God has a plan, just remember he has a seal on your life. Others will see God helping you through the tough times and know that he has a purpose for you.

Dear God, thank you for putting your stamp of approval on my life. Thank you for your special plans for me. I can trust you to carry me through the tough times. In Jesus' name, amen.

Thrive in Jesus

Be diligent in these matters; give yourself wholly to them, so that everyone may see your progress.

I TIMOTHY 4:15

Have you ever had a houseplant that seemed to grow very, very slowly? Maybe your mom or dad watered it just when they thought about it—the plant didn't get a lot of sunlight or attention. The plant wasn't dying, but it wasn't thriving either.

It's possible to be growing in your relationship with Jesus, but not thriving in it. To thrive in that relationship means that you're nurturing it—paying attention to it. You can thrive in your relationship with Jesus when you purposefully remember to do things that will make you grow. Instead of just remembering to read your Bible every once in a while, you can ask a friend to ask you how your reading's going. Instead of talking to God once a week at church, you can make a note in the front of your locker to remind you to pray between classes. When you pay attention to your relationship with God on purpose, it will do more than just grow slowly—it will thrive.

Dear God, thank you for wanting my relationship with you to thrive. Help me to give it the attention it needs so that I can grow strong in you. In Jesus' name, amen.

Trampling Your Enemies

Through you we push back our enemies; Through your name we trample our foes.

PSALM 44:5

What does it mean to trample something? It means to stomp on it! When you really want to destroy something, you can put it under your feet and smash it with your body weight.

God can help you trample your enemies under your feet. He would never want you to stomp on a person of course, but he can help you trample your everyday problems. What are you struggling with today? Is it math? Bullying? Tough emotions? Write down your problem on a piece of paper and stomp on it. When you feel like your problems are too big, remember that picture of you stamping out your problems with God's strength. God wants to help you overcome whatever's troubling you—with him, you can trample your problems under your feet!

Dear God, thank you for helping me overcome my problems. When things are tough, help me remember that just like that piece of paper, you can help me have power over my troubles. In Jesus' name, amen.

DAY 318

He Saves You All the Way

As far as The east is from The west, so far has he removed our Transgressions from us.

PSALM 103:12

If you wanted to travel halfway around the world, you'd have to go exactly 12,450.5 miles away from where you are now. The Psalmist said that as far as the east is from the west, God has taken your sin that far away from you. That's the farthest away it could possibly be!

You never have to worry that God is holding your sin against you. He doesn't sit around thinking about how disappointed he is with you for the wrong things you've done—in fact, he's erased those things from his memory. When God looks at you, he sees someone whose sin is nowhere to be found. He didn't do a halfway job when he saved you—he saved you all the way.

Dear God, thank you for saving me completely. Thank you for taking my sin and putting it so far away from me that it's like it never happened. Help me to always remember to thank you for saving me. In Jesus' name, amen.

Vengeance Is His

Do not take revenge, my dear friends, but leave room for God's wrath, for it is written: "It is mine to avenge; I will repay," says The Lord.

ROMANS 12:19

When someone does something nice for us, we often wish we could repay their kindness. It goes the other way around too—when someone does something mean to us, we may want to do something mean back. That's called taking vengeance.

God says you don't have to worry about taking vengeance on someone who has hurt you. He sees what happened and he will take care of it. That doesn't mean the other person will get away with what they did—God's not going to let that happen. Even when it does seem like the person who hurt you is going unpunished you can trust that God will bring justice in his own way and his own timing. You can leave the problem in his hands and know that he's watching out for you.

Dear God, thank you for taking care of me when someone else hurts me. Help me to forgive them and trust you to take care of the problem. In Jesus' name, amen.

DAY 320

Promising with Love

There is no fear in Love. But perfect Love drives out fear, because fear has to do with punishment. The one who fears is not made perfect in Love.

I John 4:18

Have you ever heard of a contract? It's something adults sign when they're promising to do something. For example people sign business contracts, house contracts, and car contracts saying they'll pay back the money they owe when they buy those things. These contracts can get adults in trouble if they don't keep their promises. They'll often have to pay extra money as a penalty.

It's important to keep your promises not because you might get in trouble if you break them, but because you care about the person you made a promise to. When you tell your mom you'll help her with dinner, you keep that promise out of love. When you tell your brother you'll help him with his homework, you keep that promise out of love. And when you tell your best friend you'll help her clean her room, you keep that promise out of love too. Keeping your promises out of love is much more rewarding than keeping a promise out of fear of being punished—and you'll find the other person appreciates it.

Dear God, thank you for helping me keep my promises. Help me to keep them out of love, not out of fear of being punished. Thank you for keeping your promises to me. In Jesus' name, amen.

True and False Disciples

"Not everyone who says to me, 'Lord, Lord,' will enter the kingdom of heaven, but only the one who does the will of my Father who is in heaven."

MATTHEW 7:21

Have you ever met someone who went to church every week, but didn't act like they loved Jesus when they left church? It's almost like they forgot what they learned about loving others as soon as they got in the car to go home.

Sometimes it's possible for someone to go to church without showing love for God. Jesus said that when it's time to go to heaven, some people will tell him about all the good things they did. But because they didn't actually love Jesus, he'll have to tell them to go away from him because they weren't his followers. Loving Jesus by loving others isn't something you can just do at church—it's something you do every day of the week. Keep practicing loving others every day, and you'll be a true follower of Jesus!

Dear God, help me to not just say that I love you—help me to follow you by loving others. I want to be one of your true disciples who cares about other people. In Jesus' name, amen.

Knowing the Word

No one could say a word in reply, and from that day on no one dared to ask him any more questions.

MATTHEW 22:46

The church leaders of Jesus' day were always trying to trick him. They asked him hard questions and hoped he'd get confused and look like he didn't know what he was talking about. But Jesus knew what God's Word said, and he wasn't going to be fooled by those leaders.

When you know your Bible, you won't be stumped by the tough questions someone asks you. When you study God's Word (like by reading this book!), you begin to know exactly what God says about every topic. The more you read, the more you can answer the tough questions about the Bible that your friends may ask. No one will ever be able to trick you when you've hidden God's Word in your heart!

Dear God, help me study my Bible so I know all about you. I want to be smart about your Word so I can help answer people's questions. Thank you for giving me your Word so I can study it. In Jesus' name, amen.

Are You Ready?

It will be good for those servants whose master finds them ready, even if he comes in the middle of the night or toward daybreak.

LUKE 12:38

In Bible times when the master of a house went on a long trip, he left his most trusted servant in charge of everything. Jesus said that he is like a master going on a long trip—to heaven—and will be coming back for us some day. When he does return, he hopes we'll be taking care of his world and we'll be excited to see him!

We don't know the day or the hour Jesus will come back to earth—but we can know he'll bring us to our heavenly home. He's getting a place ready for us! It's our job to be ready for him to come back by reading his Word, praying, and telling our friends about him. We can be excited just like a servant waiting to see his master and friend again.

Dear God, thank you for loving me enough to come back for me. I can't wait to see you! In Jesus' name, amen.

Do You Know Jesus?

"I tell you, whoever publicly acknowledges me before others,
the Son of Man will also acknowledge before the angels of God."

LUKE 12:8

If someone asked you who your best friend was, would you say it out loud? Of course you would! You like your best friend and you're not ashamed to admit it.

What about if someone asked you if you love Jesus? Would you tell someone else that you're friends with Jesus even if that person didn't like Jesus himself? Some people don't believe in Jesus. But you shouldn't let that stop you from saying that he's your friend and savior. Jesus said whoever admits they know him will be saved. When you tell others about your love for Jesus, Jesus tells God and his angels about his love for you. You're special to each other and you should be excited to tell others!

Dear God, thank you for being my friend. Help me to never be ashamed of that! In Jesus' name, amen.

Was Jesus God?

"I and The Father are one."
JOHN 10:30

Jesus said he was God, but he also said he was God's son. How was it possible for him to be two different people?

Did you know that water can exist in three different forms? Water can be frozen solid (ice), liquid, or gas (vapor). No matter which way the water exists, it's still water. No matter which way God shows himself (the Father, the Son, or the Holy Spirit) he's still God. Even with this explanation, we don't completely understand the mystery of Jesus being God. It's an amazing thing that we'll eventually understand when we get to heaven.

Dear God, thank you for being so incredible—God the Father, God the Son, and God the Holy Spirit. Thank you for the way that you work in my life. In Jesus' name, amen.

Leading with Love

"Now I urge you to take some food. You need it to survive. Not one of you will lose a single hair from his head."
ACTS 27:34

When the apostle Paul was a prisoner on a ship headed for Italy, the boat reached shallow water and was about to crash. Everyone except Paul panicked. They all thought they were going to die. Instead of getting stressed, Paul told everyone to eat as much of the grain as they could, then throw the rest of the food overboard so the boat wouldn't be so heavy.

Paul could have decided that no one would listen to a prisoner. He could have kept quiet instead of speaking up and saving all the people on board. Instead, he obeyed God and calmly took charge. Like Paul, you can be leader even when you might not feel like anyone will take you seriously. God has given you everything you need to lead others with love. When you stay calm in tough situations and put others first, you can be a good leader like Paul.

Dear God, help me to be a good leader by loving others and putting them first. Thank you for teaching me to lead even when I feel afraid. In Jesus' name, amen.

Unspoken Prayers

With this in mind, be alert and always keep on praying for all the Lord's people.

EPHESIANS 6:18B

Do you ever feel afraid to pray in front of other people? You might think you won't be able to find the right words, or you might be worried that you'll sound silly. It's natural to feel a little nervous about talking in public, but you can overcome that feeling when you're ready to try. God says his spirit will teach you what to say when you pray to him.

Even if you don't feel comfortable praying in front of other people yet, you can pray silently along with the prayers of your friends and family. You don't even have to say a word! God knows exactly what you're thinking. He doesn't just hear your words—he also hears what's in your heart. Whether you feel ready to pray out loud or not, God's listening. He loves you and he loves it when you pray.

Dear God, thank you for hearing my prayers! Even when I pray silently, you know exactly what I'm saying. I love you. In Jesus' name, amen.

Never Abandoned

The LORD himself goes before you and will be with you; he will never leave you nor forsake you. Do not be afraid; do not be discouraged.

DEUTERONOMY 31:8

Sometimes things in life can happen that make us feel abandoned. Maybe a parent no longer lives with us, a friend stops wanting to hang out, or a sibling stops wanting to play. When those things happen, it can cause us to feel hurt and left behind.

When we're feeling hurt and left behind, God says we can come to him and he'll be with us. He promises to never abandon us—in fact, he'll do just the opposite. He left his comfortable home in heaven so that he could be with us forever. He never wants us to feel like no one cares. He cares more than we could ever imagine. Next time you're feeling abandoned, ask God to show you that he's with you. He'll never leave you or forsake you.

Dear God, even when I feel abandoned, you never leave me alone. I can count on you to be with me both now and forever. In Jesus' name, amen.

DAY 329

Happy Couples

Do not be yoked together with unbelievers. For what do righteousness and wickedness have in common? Or what fellowship can light have with darkness?

2 CORINTHIANS 6:14

As you get older, you'll have the chance to pick the type of person you want to date. Dating is how some people figure out what type of person they want to marry, so you should pick a person who loves Jesus and treats you well.

You shouldn't be in a rush to date (you have your whole life for that!), but you can look at older Christian couples who are happy together so you can begin to know what you like when you're ready. What do these couples have in common? Make a list of the things that you notice about their families, then start practicing treating others that same way. Maybe you like how kind they are to one another, or how they make each other laugh. In the future, when you're not sure what to look for in a date, you'll have a complete list of wonderful qualities!

Dear God, help me to be smart about who I want to date. Help me remember how important it is that my future dates know and love you, and treat me well. In Jesus' name, amen.

Better Together

God seTs The Lonely in families.
PSALM 68:6A

Have you ever gotten really busy and stressed out by school, sports, or other activities? When you're feeling that way, you might forget to make time to hang out with your family. The same thing can happen to your mom, dad, or other family members you live with—they might get busy with work or other life-stuff. It doesn't mean they've completely disappeared or forgotten you—it just means they're distracted right then.

If you feel like you haven't connected with your family for a while because they're busy, try telling them how you feel. Chances are, they'd love to hang out. Ask how you can help them feel less stressed so you can make time for each other. God put you in a family because you need each other!

Dear God, help me remember to make time for my family. Help me to tell my family when I miss them and want to hang out. Thank you for making us better together! In Jesus' name, amen.

Tricky Asking

Therefore each of you must put off falsehood and speak truthfully.

EPHESIANS 4:25A

Sometimes one of the adults in your house might say no when you wish they'd say yes. Maybe you'd like to have a friend over, watch more television, or eat more dessert. If a parent tells you no, it might be tempting to find another adult in your house and ask them to say yes. That's being tricky.

When your parents tell you no about something, there's usually a good reason. Instead of trying to trick them into saying yes, respectfully ask your parent to explain their reasons and if they'd think about changing their mind. You can explain why you'd like to do what you're asking. If they say no again, do your best to know that they want what's best to keep you healthy and happy. There will be other times you might get to do what you're asking—but for now you should trust that your parent loves you and wants what's best for you.

Dear God, help me to accept that my parents are trying to do what's best for me. I don't want to try to trick them into giving me what I want. Thank you for giving me a family who cares for me. In Jesus' name, amen.

Looking for Something Similar

Live in harmony with one another.
ROMANS 12:16A

Have you ever had someone hang out with you at an event until other people showed up—then everyone ignored you? How did that make you feel? It's normal to be excited when someone new shows up at church, school, or a party—but it's important to make sure that you don't forget about the people who were there first.

When you're introducing people at an event or at school, think about what they might have in common—then ask them about it. Do they both play sports? Do they like the same types of video games? Or do they both like to the same restaurants? Trying to find similarities between your friends' lives will help everyone feel more comfortable. Before you know it, they'll be talking and having a good time and so will you. A good friend is a person who knows how to help everyone feel included. How can you include someone today?

Dear God, help me remember to include everyone who visits my church, school, and other events. I want to be a good friend. In Jesus' name, amen.

DAY 333

Saving for Others

"You expected much, but see, it turned out to be little. What you brought home, I blew away. Why?" declares the LORD ALMIGHTY. "Because of my house, which remains a ruin, while each of you is busy with your own house."

HAGGAI 1:9

When God told his children to save for their futures, he also wanted them to include saving things for others who had nothing for themselves. In fact, the Bible often tells us that we should help people who are less well-off than we are.

When you're saving money for things you want or need, don't forget to put a little aside for others who may not be able to buy things for themselves. After you're done saving for yourself and others, give that money through a special program at church, to a local shelter, or to a charity (with your parents' approval). God has blessed you with so much, and he wants you to use some of what you have to bless others.

Dear God, thank you for helping me to save for my future, as well as to save some to share with others. In Jesus' name, amen.

Why We Don't Make Sacrifices Anymore

So Christ was sacrificed once to take away the sins of many.
HEBREWS 9:28A

In the Old Testament times when people did something wrong, they brought an offering to the temple and confessed their sin. People offered up animals, food, wealth, and other possessions. This kind of sacrificing happened before Jesus came to live among us.

We don't make sacrifices like this at church anymore—Jesus was the perfect sacrifice. When he died on the cross and came back to life so we could be forgiven, he was the last sacrifice that ever needed to be made. Now church is no longer a place of sacrifice and sadness, but a place of forgiveness and joy. We can be thankful every time we go to church that Jesus sacrificed himself for us!

Dear God, thank you for sending Jesus as the perfect sacrifice for my sin. Thank you for making church a place of happiness and joy for me! In Jesus' name, amen.

Working Hard When No One's Watching

Go to the ant, you sluggard; consider its ways and be wise! It has no commander, no overseer or ruler, yet it stores its provisions in summer and gathers its food at harvest.

PROVERBS 6:6–8

When you work hard on your homework even when no one's home to make you, your hard work helps on the pop quiz the next day. When you do extra chores so you can save some money, your work will pay off when you can buy what you want later. And when you practice shooting hoops even though the game isn't until Saturday, your work will show on the court.

Sometimes we have to work hard now, even though we won't see the results until much later. The Bible says even tiny ants know to work hard before winter comes so they'll have enough food to make it through the cold season. You can be encouraged that even when you think no one's watching, your hard work is going to pay off!

Dear God, help me to work hard even when no one's watching. Help me remember that I'm working so that I can have good things in my future. In Jesus' name, amen.

Staying Strong

Therefore I will boast all the more gladly about my weaknesses, so that Christ's power may rest on me.

2 CORINTHIANS 12:9B

Sometimes when you're feeling weak, God wants to show his power through you. You might not feel like you can make it through the school day or that you cannot complete your homework because you're really tired. Or you might not feel like you have one more minute of patience with your brother or sister because you're so worn down.

Paul was one of the first and greatest followers of Jesus. But even he sometimes felt like he had weaknesses. When you're feeling like you can't be strong anymore, know that you aren't alone. Even the amazing apostle Paul knew what it was like to feel like he couldn't complete a difficult task sometimes. God showed his power through him, though, and Paul did great things with God's strength.

Dear God, thank you for being with me when I feel weak. Thank you for giving me power to do the work I need to do. I love you. In Jesus' name, amen.

Encouraging New Christians

For you know That we dealT wiTh each of you as a faTher deals wiTh his own children, encouraging, comforTing and urging you To Live Lives worThy of God, who calls you inTo his kingdom and glory.

1 THESSALONIANS 2:11-12

When someone you know becomes a member of God's family, that person needs help getting to know Jesus better. The apostle Paul knew this, so when he met new Christians he treated them kindly as he taught them about the Bible. He loved these new Christians so much that he said he felt like a new parent.

The new members of God's family are counting on you to love them like Paul loved his new family. When you're excited about something you learned about in the Bible, tell your new Christian friends about it. When God answers your prayers, tell them about that too. When they're having a hard time, listen to them and care about how they're feeling. All of these things will help them get to know Jesus better. God's given you a special ability to love the people who have just come into his family—how will you do that today?

Dear God, help me to love others as they get to know you better. I want to help others grow in what they know about you. In Jesus' name, amen.

God's Discipline

No discipline seems pleasant at the time, but painful. Later on, however, it produces a harvest of righteousness and peace for those who have been trained by it.

HEBREWS 12:11

It might not feel good when your parents discipline you—you might not like being grounded, missing out on television, or skipping a soccer game. Your parents are using discipline to get your attention, though. They want you to stop and think before you do something that might hurt you or someone else.

God disciplines you sometimes too. He doesn't do it because he wants you to be miserable. He does it because he wants to get your attention—to make sure you're living in a way that's safe for you and others. He might discipline you by letting you fail a test if you didn't study or getting in trouble with your parents when you break their rules. God has a lot of ways to get your attention, and he does it because he wants you to make a change. So next time you feel like he's trying to get your attention, stop and think what you can learn from him.

Dear God, help me to pay attention when you're trying to stop me from causing harm. Thank you for loving me enough to discipline me. In Jesus' name, amen.

DAY 339

Finishing Strong

LeT perseverance finish iTs work so ThaT you may be maTure and compLeTe, noT Lacking anyThing.

JAMES 1:4

A track runner might start a race in first place and go fast at first, passing all the other participants. But if the athlete pushes too hard in the beginning of the race, he or she might run out of strength before the race is over. Runners need to practice something called "pacing".

Your life is like a race. You need to pace yourself. You have a lot going on—schoolwork, volunteering, and after-school activities. Take a few minutes every day to pace yourself. Stop and take some deep breaths. When you get overwhelmed, take a five-minute break to clear your head. When you take those few minutes for yourself, you will get the energy you need to come back and finish your day strong for Jesus.

What's your day been like? Is there something that's overwhelming you? When can you schedule five minutes to sit and take a break so you can feel ready to go again?

God as Your King

But the people refused to listen to Samuel. "No!" they said. "We want a king over us. Then we will be like all the other nations, with a king to lead us and to go out before us and fight our battles."

I Samuel 8:19–20

When God's people first asked for a king, they did it because they wanted to be like other nations. God gave them what they wanted, but it made him sad—he had always been their king. God was wiser and more powerful than any human leader could be.

We should always respect our leaders, but we know that God is our ultimate king. He takes the best care of us because he knows us the best. So when you feel disappointed because someone let you down, remember that God hasn't forgotten you. He's the best king you could ever have.

Dear God, as my king you take care of me. When others disappoint me, help me remember to look to you as my help. In Jesus' name, amen

The Bible for Others

They read from The Book of The Law of God, making
iT cLear and giving The meaning So ThaT The peopLe
underStood whaT waS being read.

NEHEMIAH 8:8

In Old Testament times, the prophet Ezra had to explain the Bible to God's people. There were a lot of words in scripture that people didn't understand—the Bible wasn't written in the language they spoke at the time.

Today we read the Bible in our own language, but it hasn't always been translated into English. A long time ago, some people took the time to translate it so that we could read God's Word for ourselves. There are still people around the world who don't have a copy of the Bible in their own language, though. Missionaries are working to translate God's Word for them, but sometimes that job takes years. While those people are waiting to hear God's Word in their language, we can pray for them. We can ask God to prepare their hearts so they'll be ready to hear and understand what he wants them to know.

Dear God, thank you for giving me a Bible I can read and understand in my own language. I pray that you'll bring your Word to people around the world. In Jesus' name, amen.

Saying Thanks

That night the king could not sleep; so he ordered the book of the chronicles, the record of his reign, to be brought in and read to him.

ESTHER 6:1

One night King Xerxes couldn't sleep. He was hoping to fall asleep while being read to—so he asked someone to bring out the record of things that had happened while he was king. The list was long, but one thing he noticed was that a man named Mordecai had saved the king's life, but the king had forgotten to reward him for that amazing deed.

Sometimes someone you need to thank might come to your mind. You could be trying to sleep, or be in the middle of your school day. When you remember that person's good deed, thank them for what they did for you as soon as you can. Write an email, make a card, or tell them thank you with your words. God has brought that person to your mind for a reason, and you can be an encouragement to him just by saying thank you.

Dear God, help me remember to thank those who have made a difference in my life—big or small. Thank you for surrounding me with people who help me. In Jesus' name, amen.

God is I Am

BUT Moses said To God, "Who am I That I should go To Pharaoh and bring The Israelites ouT of EgypT?"
Exodus 3:11

God had a special plan for Moses from the day he was born. Moses was chosen to rescue God's people from Egypt where they were slaves. But when Moses realized what God wanted him to do, he felt afraid. He asked God, "Who am I that I should go to Pharaoh and bring the Israelites out of Egypt?" God replied, "This is what you are to say to the Israelites: 'I AM has sent me to you.'"

I am is another name for God. God was telling Moses that it didn't matter how important Moses seemed or did not seem—it only mattered how important God was. When you feel afraid or like you don't have what it takes to follow God's plan for your life, remember that it isn't about how big or strong you are—it's about how big and strong God is. You can do anything he asks of you with him on your side.

Dear God, thank you for being powerful enough to work out your plan in my life. I trust you and choose to follow your directions. In Jesus' name, amen.

Wise Friends

After the death of Jehoiada, the officials of Judah came and paid homage to the king, and he listened to them. They abandoned the temple of the Lord.

2 CHRONICLES 24:17-18A

When Joash first became king of Israel, it seemed like he was doing a good job. He told people to worship and obey God, and he worshiped and obeyed God too. But when the priest who gave Joash advice died, Joash started to take advice from people who didn't love God. Soon the whole nation was living in wickedness because King Joash was listening to the wrong people.

It's really important that we take our advice from people who love God and want the best for us. Sunday school teachers, parents, and friends who are Christians are a great place to start. When someone tells us to do something that doesn't sound like it would honor God, we should look in the Bible and ask other Christians what the right thing to do would be. When we look for advice from the right people, we can know that we're headed in the right direction!

Dear God, help me to be careful about where I get my advice. Help me remember that others are watching how I live, just like others watched Joash and the way he lived. I want to honor you in everything I do. In Jesus' name, amen.

When Times Get Tough

I will proclaim the name of the Lord. Oh, praise the greatness of our God!

DEUTERONOMY 32:3

Sometimes when you're having a particularly bad day, it's hard to remember that things haven't always been hard. You've had good days too! It's important during the hard days to have a way to remember how God has taken care of you in the past.

When the nation of Israel was going through a hard time, Moses taught them a song about their past. The song reminded the people of everything God had brought them through. Maybe next time you're going through a tough time, you can sing a praise song from church or even write one of your own. Write down the things God has done for you and ask for faith to believe God is going to bring you through difficult days to happier times again.

Dear God, you take care of me during both good and tough days. Help me remember to look back and see how you've taken care of me in the past. Thank you for helping me look forward to good days again. In Jesus' name, amen.

Taking Communion

And he took the bread, gave thanks and broke it, and gave it to them, saying, "This is my body given for you; do this in remembrance of me."

LUKE 22:19

Some churches have a part of the service that's called communion, the Lord's Supper, or the Eucharist. During this special part of the church service, people eat bread and drink grape juice or wine. While they're doing this, they are remembering the last supper that Jesus had with his disciples before he died. During that supper, Jesus said that every time they ate bread and drank wine in the future, they could remember and thank him for his sacrifice for them. He said his body was like bread that was broken and the wine was like his blood poured out for those who believe in him.

Any time you're eating bread or drinking juice, you can think about how Jesus had communion with his disciples. Take a minute to thank him for the sacrifice he made for you.

Dear God, help me to always remember your sacrifice for me. Thank you for giving your life so that I can have a relationship with you. In Jesus' name, amen.

Is Sickness a Punishment?

His disciples asked him, "Rabbi, who sinned, this man or his
parents, that he was born blind?" "Neither this man nor his
parents sinned," said Jesus, "but this happened so that the works
of God might be displayed in him."

JOHN 9:2–3

Back in Jesus' time, some people believed that if a person was sick it was punishment for something wrong they had done. Jesus showed that being sick doesn't have to do with punishment at all—we don't really know why people get sick—only God does.

If someone you love is sick, remember that person needs your love. If you're the one who's sick, you'd appreciate it if someone visits you or sends a card saying they care. If someone you know is sick, you can think of similar things to do for them. Sickness is no fun, but it's a chance to receive or show kindness to someone who needs to be encouraged.

Dear God, I don't understand why anyone gets sick. But help me to think of ways I can show love to others who are not well. In Jesus' name, amen.

Following the Law

Jesus replied: "'Love The Lord your God wiTh all your heart and with all your soul and wiTh all your mind.'"

MATTHEW 22:37

Sometimes it might seem like the Bible has a lot of instructions. Those instructions are in God's Word so that we know how to live safe and happy lives. God wants us to do our best to obey what he tells us in the Bible. Not just because he tells us to but because we love him.

When we love God, obeying him becomes much easier. Being kind to others, sharing what we have, worshiping him—all of these things are things we want to do when there's love for God in our hearts. How can you show that love for him today?

Dear God, help me to follow the rules not just because I should, but because I love you. Put love in my heart for you. In Jesus' name, amen.

Loving Littler Kids

If anyone causes one of these little ones—who believes in
me—to stumble, it would be better for them if a large millstone
were hung around their neck and they were thrown into the sea.
MARK 9:42

Sometimes when someone's younger than you, it might be tempting to think they're not able to understand as much about God as you do. While it's true that the older you get the more you can understand about God, it's also important to never make a younger child feel like he or she is too small to have a friendship with Jesus.

Little kids can have big faith. Encourage the little ones in your life to tell you what they're learning about God in church or at home. It helps them grow in their friendship with Jesus when they get to talk about their faith. By listening to what they're learning, you're helping them know that they're important to God, and they can enjoy a friendship with him just like you do.

Dear God, help me remember that little kids can have big faith. Help me to be a good listener so I can help the little ones around me have faith in you. In Jesus' name, amen.

DAY 350

Fearing God

The fear of The Lord is The beginning of wisdom.
PSALM 111:10A

Did you know the Bible says we should fear God? That doesn't mean we should be *afraid* of God, it means that we should be respectful when we think about how powerful he is. Since he was powerful enough to create the world and hold together everything in it, he deserves our respect.

When we fear God—when we show him respect—it means we obey him. When he says we should treat others with love, help the poor, and obey our parents, we show him respect. There are many ways you can show respect to God—what's one way you can do that today?

Dear God, help me show you respect. You deserve all the respect I can give. I love you. In Jesus' name, amen.

Leading the Way

Now Deborah, a prophet, the wife of Lappidoth, was leading Israel at the time.

JUDGES 4:4

It's important to know that whether you're a girl or boy, God has a special job for you. Deborah is an example of a woman who served God in a big way—she worked as a leader of God's people, and later helped lead the Israelites in war. David is an example of a man who served God by being king and by leading the army. Whoever you are, you can have an important part in what God is doing.

Look at the men and women in your church and where you live—what things are they doing to serve God? What are some ways you think God wants you to serve others? God made you to serve him in big ways. How can you be a leader today?

Dear God, thank you for giving me the chance to love and to lead other people right where I am. Please show me how to do that. In Jesus' name, amen.

The Judgment of God

The dead were judged according to what they had done as recorded in the books.

REVELATION 20:12B

If someone breaks the law and has to go to court, would it be okay for the judge to tell the person who broke the law, "Never mind—it's okay to break the law every once in a while"? No, the judge would probably never say that because it's his or her job to enforce the law.

God is like a judge—he knows when we do something right and when we do something wrong. Only Jesus is perfect—we humans all make mistakes. That's why Jesus died for us and took away our sin. But Jesus' sacrifice doesn't mean we can sin all we want. It means we get a second chance, a way to be forgiven when we mess up and tell God we're sorry.

God doesn't overlook our sins—he doesn't think it's okay to break the law. But he does love us, and he always wants us to make good choices that make us more like Jesus.

Dear God, even though you have to enforce the law, you made a way for me to be forgiven. Thank you for sending Jesus to die for my sins. In Jesus' name, amen.

DAY 353

When Others Steal

That night the Lord appeared to him and said, "I am the God of your father Abraham. Do not be afraid, for I am with you."

GENESIS 26:24A

Isaac lived in a dry place where finding water was difficult. He dug a well, but some of his enemies came and took it from him. He dug another well, and they took that one too. Every time he dug a well, he let other people steal it instead of standing up for himself.

Is there someone in your life you need to stand up against? Does someone at school take your lunch, your gym clothes, or your backpack? It's not okay for people to take what belongs to you. Talk to your friends and the adults at school and ask for help in standing up for yourself. It's the only way they'll learn that they can't get away with taking what isn't theirs. God is with you.

Dear God, help me to stand up against people who take things from me or from others. Let me be like Isaac who learned how to defend what he'd worked hard to have. In Jesus' name, amen.

It's Not Fair

Yet I will rejoice in The Lord, I will be joyful in God my Savior.
HABAKKUK 3:18

Sometimes life isn't going to feel fair. Someone else might get what you want. Your brother, sister, or friend might take the bigger slice of cake, or someone might skip ahead of you in line when you've been waiting a long time.

You can tell the other person how you feel. They might not understand or decide to be fair, but you'll feel better because you used your words to tell them what's going on with your feelings. Even when things don't turn out to be fair in your opinion, remember that even Jesus knows what it's like to be treated unfairly. People punished him for something he didn't do—he died on the cross for sins that weren't his. When you feel you are being treated unfairly, talk to God. He's right there with you. He can help you feel better and he knows exactly what you're going through.

Dear God, when things don't seem fair, you still care about me. Help me to treat others with kindness even when they don't treat me in a way that's nice. In Jesus' name, amen.

Calming Down

A hoT-Tempered person sTirs up conflicT, buT The one who is paTienT calms a quarrel.

PROVERBS 15:18

Sometimes when someone is angry or sad and they don't want to talk, the best thing you can do is give them a few minutes to calm down. If your brother is mad because you got to go to a friend's house and he had to stay home, he might need some time to calm down. Or if a friend is upset because you did better on a test than she, she might need some space.

It's okay for your friends and family to need a little time before they feel better. Even if what happened wasn't your fault, the Bible says speaking kindly to someone helps people feel better. So next time someone is angry, try speaking kindly or just saying nothing for a while. Before you know it, they'll be feeling like themselves again and everything will be okay.

Dear God, with a little time and space people can feel better again. Help me to know when to use kind words and when to keep quiet for a while. In Jesus' name, amen.

No Shame in Worship

Then Mary took about a pint of pure nard, an expensive perfume; she poured it on Jesus' feet and wiped his feet with her hair. And the house was filled with the fragrance of the perfume.

JOHN 12:3

Not long before Jesus died, a woman named Mary brought an expensive bottle of perfume to the place where Jesus was and poured it on Jesus' feet. The perfume cost more than one year's hard work. Some people judged Mary for wasting the perfume when she could have given the money to the poor, but Mary was worshiping Jesus by what she did.

Like Mary, you don't need to be ashamed of the way you choose to worship Jesus. You can do it quietly or loudly. You can sing or dance. You can worship him by secretly doing good deeds, or you can inspire others by being a leader in front of the church. However you choose to worship Jesus, he's honored by your heart for him.

Dear God, whatever my style of worship is, you're happy that I'm worshiping you. Help me show you honor in everything I do. I love you. In Jesus' name, amen.

God as Redeemer

They remembered That God was Their Rock, That God Most High was Their Redeemer.

PSALM 78:35

Sometimes things happen that don't make sense. You might lose someone you love, have a really hard time in school, or watch your family split apart. When something bad happens, it's hard to imagine that things will ever feel okay again.

God promises he won't waste any of the problems you go through. It breaks his heart to see when life is tough for you, but he promises he'll stick with you and in the end he'll redeem your life—he'll make something new out of it. When others see that you've made it through a rough time, they'll know they can trust God to bring them through their problems too. What problems can you trust God to redeem—make new—for you?

Dear God, you make my life new again, even after tough times. Thank you for never leaving me or forsaking me. In Jesus' name, amen.

DAY 358

Emotions as Warnings

And The peace of God, which Transcends all understanding, will guard your hearts and your minds in Christ Jesus.
PHILIPPIANS 4:7

Have you ever noticed the lights on a car dashboard when something's wrong with the engine? Those lights are there to warn you to pull the car over and check on it before something even worse happens.

Your emotions—your feelings—are like the lights on a car dashboard. When you feel yourself getting angry, step away and think about what you need to do next. When you're feeling sad, find someone to talk to or a quiet place where you can calm down. When you're feeling jealous, stop and pray that God will help you treat the other person with kindness instead of envy.

Emotions are an important part of who you are. They give you the chance to pause and think before you do something you might regret later.

Dear God, thank you for giving me emotions. Thank you for this warning sign that tells me to slow down and think about what I'll do next. Help me to use my emotions for good. In Jesus' name, amen.

DAY 359

Family Peace

Make every effort To Live in peace with everyone.
HEBREWS 12:14A

Did you ever notice how even families in the Bible had problems? Joseph's brothers were so jealous of him that they tried to kill him. Jacob stole Esau's inheritance. From the beginning of time, some families have had a hard time getting along.

Is there someone in your family who can really get on your nerves? What can you do to try to make peace with that person? Maybe you could spend some time doing fun things with them. Maybe you could pray for them or ask an adult to help you figure out how to love the person who's bothering you.

Family is a gift from God, but sometimes during tough times it's hard to figure out how to get along with each other. When you need help with that, ask God and ask an adult to help you make peace.

Dear God, thank you for my family. Help me figure out how to be at peace with people who are sometimes difficult. I want to love the family you've given me. In Jesus' name, amen.

Coming Near to God

Come near to God and he will come near to you.
JAMES 4:8A

Sometimes it can feel like God's a long way away. Life gets busy or something tough happens, and it's hard to feel he's there. Every once in a while, David even said that God seemed to hide his face from him. That didn't mean God wasn't there—it just meant David couldn't sense him nearby.

When God feels far away, know that he hasn't left you. You can keep having faith that he's right there with you, taking care of you. The Bible says that when you draw near to God, he'll draw near to you. You might not know he's there right away, but eventually he'll show you he's been with you all along. When things are tough, hang in there. God has your back and he's not leaving your side.

Dear God, when I have a hard time feeling you near I must remember you're still here with me. Thank you for always taking care of me. I love you. In Jesus' name, amen.

Devotion to Prayer

Devote yourselves to prayer, being watchful and thankful.
COLOSSIANS 4:2

When you're devoted to your favorite sport, that means you enjoy practicing and playing it. When you're devoted to a friend, that means you want to spend all your time with that person. When you're devoted to your favorite school subject, that means you want to read everything you can about it.

God says there's something even more awesome you can be devoted to—prayer. That doesn't mean you have to be on your knees with your eyes closed all day (how would you get anything else done?). It just means that whatever you're doing, you can talk to God about it. Walking to the bus stop? Tell him what you're thankful for. Having trouble with a friend? Ask him to help you. Worried about your family? You can pray about that too. God wants to hear from you any time at all—he wants you to be devoted to prayer.

Dear God, thank you for helping me be devoted to prayer. Thank you for wanting to hear from me about anything at any time! I love you. In Jesus' name, amen.

Fruits of the Spirit

BuT The fruiT of The SpiriT is Love, joy, peace, forbearance,
kindness, goodness, faiThfulness, genTleness and self-conTrol.
AgainsT such Things There is no Law.
GALATIANS 5:22–23

When you bite into a big juicy piece of fruit, it's hard to believe sometimes how delicious it tastes. But the fruit didn't start out that
way—most fruit tastes bitter until it has had time to ripen. It has to grow
into something you'll want to eat and share with others.

God says that he's growing good fruit in your life—not the kind you
put in your mouth, but the kind you put in your heart. He's growing a
good, sweet attitude in you. When things get tough and you're having
trouble with your attitude, he can help you find a way to be sweet. When
you have a good attitude, everything starts to feel a little better—and
others will appreciate being around your sweet spirit.

Dear God, thank you for helping me with my attitude. Next time I'm
having trouble because I haven't gotten my way, help me to ask you for
the attitude that pleases you. In Jesus' name, amen.

Under His Wings

He will cover you with his feathers, and under his wings you will find refuge.

PSALM 91:4A

When a mama bird wants to protect her young from a storm, she spreads out her wings and covers them. The little birds can sleep under those wings knowing that nothing can hurt them or make them afraid.

God says he's like your parent-bird. He's protecting you—watching over you while you sleep, eat, do homework, and play. When you're feeling anxious or afraid because of what's going on in your life, ask him to help you feel better. His wings are covering you—you can rest in his protection.

Dear God, thank you for protecting me when I feel anxious or afraid. Thank you for keeping me safe. In Jesus' name, amen.

DAY 364

You're Making a Difference

ALways give yourseLves fuLLy To The work of The Lord, because
you know ThaT your Labor in The Lord is noT in vain.
I CORINTHIANS 15:58B

What does your day look like? Do you get up? Get on the bus? Get to class? Those might seem like ordinary things, but did you know that with every step you take you can make a difference for someone?

When you smile at someone on the bus, you've brought them happiness. When you thank the lunch line worker, you've brought them joy. When you bring in your best homework, you've shown your teacher you're listening.

Everything you do—even the ordinary things—brings happiness to someone else. You are making a difference just by showing up for your life. God promises that because you're loving other people, he'll reward you. He sees your good attitude and he's proud of you.

Dear God, thank you for helping me make a difference for the people in my life. Thank you for using even the small stuff to bring big happiness to someone else. Help me remember to keep serving you in the little ways. In Jesus' name, amen

The Adventure Begins

LeT us draw near To God wiTh a sincere hearT and wiTh The fuLL assurance ThaT faiTh brings.

HEBREWS 10:22A

Y ou made it! You spent 365 days on an adventure with God. You picked up this book 365 times! The coolest part is, there's even more adventure ahead of you.

Don't let your exciting journey stop here. You can open this book up at Day 1 and start it all over again—but it won't be the same. Next time around, you'll notice things you didn't notice the first time you read this devotional—things that could change your journey. You'll have more conversations with God. You'll have more excitement as you share his Word with others. And you'll know God even better!

So go ahead—take this challenge. Don't let the last page be the end of your adventure with God.

Dear God, we've had an awesome adventure together. Let's not stop here—help me to keep following you on the great adventure you have planned for my life. In Jesus' name, amen.

Scriptural Index

Topical Index

NIV Adventure Bible, Polar Exploration Edition,
Hardcover, Full Color

With over 9 million copies sold, the Adventure Bible brand is beloved by Christian schools, churches, and families alike. Now, the #1 Bible for kids, including all of its trusted essentials loved by parents, is available in an exciting polar exploration theme!

Ready for a frosty adventure? Embark on a fun, exciting trek through God's Word with the NIV Adventure Bible, now in an all-new polar exploration theme! While on this arctic adventure, readers meet all types of people, see all sorts of places, and learn all kinds of facts about the Bible. And most importantly you'll grow closer in your relationship with God.

Features of the *NIV Adventure Bible, Polar Exploration Edition* include:

- The same trusted Adventure Bible content in a frosty new theme
- Full-color images of polar animals, arctic outposts, and icy landscapes throughout make learning about the Bible even more engaging
- Life in Bible Times—Articles and illustrations describe what life was like in ancient days
- Words to Treasure—Highlights great verses to memorize
- Did You Know?—Interesting facts help you understand God's Word and the life of faith
- People in Bible Times—Articles offer close-up looks at amazing people of the Bible
- Live It! Hands-on activities help you apply biblical truths to your life
- Twenty polar-themed pages focus on topics such as how to know you are a Christian, famous people of the Bible, highlights of the life of Jesus, and how to pray.
- Book introductions feature arctic art and important information about each book of the Bible
- Dictionary/concordance for looking up tricky words
- Color map section to help locate places in the Bible
- Complete text of the New International Version (NIV) of the Bible
- Thrilling new glacial cover on metallic paper
- The NIV Adventure Bible is recommended by more Christian schools and churches than any other Bible for kids!

Available in stores and online!